Praise for *Farewell*

"Intimate astonishments jump out—like fish breaking the surface of a still, dark lake from Foote's quiet, warm, dignified narrative. . . . If you are new to Foote, *Farewell* may prompt you to explore his distinguished body of work. When the 16-year-old Horton boards the bus for Dallas and acting school, and bids farewell to Wharton, you may find yourself impatient for another installment of his long and well-lived life."

—Dan Hulbert, *The Atlanta Journal-Constitution*

"His tales, most of them set in the Texas of his childhood, unfold with the slow, easy grace of a flower opening to the sun. . . . But by the end of the all-too-brief, beautifully written volume, Foote's relations feel like our family, and Foote's memories of life in the segregated South before and during the Great Depression seem more vivid than any of our own."

—Jack Helbig, *Booklist*

"Not surprisingly, Foote writes prose as beautifully as he crafts the dialog that has earned him Academy Awards for the screenplays of *To Kill a Mockingbird* and *Tender Mercies* and a Pulitzer Prize for his play *The Young Man from Atlanta*. . . . Foote's memoir is a loving and gentle recollection that every library will want."

—Barry X. Miller, *Library Journal*

"In *Farewell*, Horton Foote turns to the actual people and events that lie behind so many of his plays—the apparently peaceful but land-mined surroundings of his childhood in Texas. The whole account is rich in Foote's most striking skills—the brisk clarity of his memory and the uncanny ability of his plain language to summon the urgent human complexities."

—Reynolds Price, author of *Roxanna Slade*

"Poignant, mirthful, eccentric and deeply loving, Horton Foote's people mirror the Depression years of the South when the small town was at its zenith. Here, as in many of his plays, he preserves for us a society which, with all its inequities, was a unique part of America. A beautiful work."

—Harper Lee, author of *To Kill a Mockingbird*

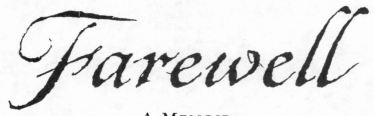

Farewell

A MEMOIR
OF A TEXAS CHILDHOOD

HORTON FOOTE

A TOUCHSTONE BOOK
PUBLISHED BY SIMON & SCHUSTER
NEW YORK LONDON TORONTO SYDNEY SINGAPORE

TOUCHSTONE
Rockefeller Center
1230 Avenue of the Americas
New York, NY 10020

Copyright © 1999 by Sunday Rock Corp.
All rights reserved,
including the right of reproduction
in whole or in part in any form.
First Touchstone Edition 2000
TOUCHSTONE and colophon are registered trademarks of Simon & Schuster, Inc.

Designed by Colin Joh
Set in Garamond

Manufactured in the United States of America

1 3 5 7 9 10 8 6 4 2

The Library of Congress has cataloged the Scribner edition as follows:
Foote, Horton.
Farewell: a memoir of a Texas childhood/Horton Foote.
p. cm.
1. Foote, Horton—Childhood and youth. 2. Dramatists, American—20th century—Biography.
3. Screenwriters—United States—Biography. 4. Foote, Horton—Homes and haunts—Texas.
5.Texas—Social life and customs. 6. Family—Texas. I. Title.
PS3511.O344Z468   1999
812'.54—dc21[B]   99-10227
CIP

ISBN 0-684-84439-7
0-684-86570-X (Pbk)

In memory of my wife, Lillian Vallish Foote

Author's Note

Having kept no diary or journal, I've had to rely entirely on my memory of my childhood and youth, or what I remember being told of events before I was born, except for a few letters or newspaper clippings saved by me or my family.

Part I

*Here I am at age three. The first child
in my generation, I was born into
an extended family of grandparents,
great-aunts, great-uncles, aunts,
uncles, cousins and great storytellers.*

Chapter 1

I left my home in Wharton at sixteen, but no matter how poor I was, and I was often very poor, I always managed to return for a visit at least once a year, and whenever I met with friends or relatives on those visits we inevitably got around to: "Do you remember when," or "I wonder whatever happened to . . ."

I was the first grandchild born into the extended family that surrounded me in Wharton and Houston. On my father's side I had a grandmother, a stepgrandfather, an aunt, three great-aunts, a great-uncle, a great-great-uncle and first, second and third cousins in abundance. On my mother's side I had a grandfather, grandmother, two aunts, three uncles, three great-uncles, four great-aunts and many first, second and third cousins. Also, nearer the coast in the towns of East Columbia and Angleton were other great-aunts and cousins.

I was fond of all of them, and particularly close to my mother's mother and father, her younger sisters and her brothers. The backyards of our houses joined and we were always, it seemed to me, visiting each other.

Whenever my mother and her sisters got together, sooner or

later, one of them would ask: "I wonder why the boys [meaning their brothers] are like they are?"

As the years went on the questions were somewhat rephrased, and became more concerned and urgent, because by then the boys, now grown men, had begun in earnest their wasted, tragic lives. Wasted tragic lives, I had by twelve observed, seemed nearly always to occur to at least one male member of the families we knew, but to have the only three sons of a family turn out so was most unusual. The town, too, seemed to realize how unusual it was, and for many years seemed as obsessed with that question as we were. For my family learned from well-meaning friends that it was out of our hearing a much discussed topic, and to our faces, from time to time, each of us was asked the question, put in a studied, casual, offhand way, "What has happened to the Brooks boys?" or "Where are the Brooks boys now?" or "Do you stay in touch with the Brooks boys?"

I seldom hear that question now, because my father and mother and her immediate family are all dead and except for two cousins that live in Houston, anyone else related to the boys (as we continued calling them even when two of them lived to their early sixties) are dead, too, as well as any friends that knew them. When I visit with the cousin from Houston who remembers them as vividly as I do, we will still at some point ask once again, "I wonder why the boys turned out the way they did?"

Fifteen, or ten years ago, even, a number of people living in Wharton would have known them, or heard of them through their parents. They would have known, too, that the handsome, stately house on Richmond Road, now visibly neglected, with the huge cypress tree shading the front gallery, and the fruit market and general store to one side of its front yard, had once been owned by the Brookses, and was still called the Brooks house, although it had been owned for fifty years by another family, the owners of the fruit market and the general store.

I thought of the Brooks boys recently when I was sent a picture taken in 1928 of my eighth-grade class. I remember well all but four of my classmates pictured there, know in some measure what happened to those I remember and realize that none of them that are living any longer live in Wharton so that even if I wanted to ask again what happened to so-and-so, or do you remember when—there is no one in town I could ask these questions, or no one to ask me about the Brooks boys.

I was the youngest in my class and in the picture almost every girl is at least a head taller. It occurred to me that this slight young fellow (still eleven years old—twelve in March) had already decided he wanted to be an actor, although it was still only a secret wish confided to few people. I had told my mother and father and overheard them one night on their front gallery— my father always called it the gallery, my mother usually referred to it as a porch—discussing this desire, "notion," they called it, and reassuring themselves that I would grow out of it. I didn't. Indeed the determination grew stronger each year thereafter, so that when I graduated from high school, at sixteen, I refused to even consider going to college and insisted that my Depression-burdened parents send me to New York to a dramatic school, which they did, though first insisting that I wait a year to be sure it was still what I wanted to do, and then substituting Pasadena Playhouse in Pasadena, California, for New York, "You are too young to be turned loose in New York, Son."

The only plays I'd seen were those performed by the Dude Arthur Comedians, a tent show that came to our town once a year for a week, Florence Reed in a stock company production of *The Shanghai Gesture* in Houston, Vilma Banky and Rod La Roque (two film stars whose careers had been ruined by the advent of talking pictures) in a touring production of *Cherries Are Ripe,* also in Houston. Then, too, there was the Wharton Little Theatre, formed when I was a freshman in high school, and where I saw productions of *Coquette, The Silver Cord, Sun Up, Enter Madame,* George Kelly's *The Torch-Bearers* and a melodrama, *Gold in Them Thar Hills.*

When I was a sophomore, Eppie Murphree, just graduated from college, came to Wharton to teach speech and put on plays in high school. I found a way to tell her my ambition to be an actor, and, to my relief, she took it very seriously. She cast me that spring in a one-act play, about three college roommates, one of them having a serious drug problem. I was cast as the young addict. I knew a lady in town that I was told was addicted to paregoric, but that was the extent of my knowledge of drug use. However I got my ideas for the behavior of this young man (there is a scene in which he confesses to his unsuspecting roommates that he is an addict and has a kind of fit before them, since he needs a fix and he has no money for drugs), it must have had some effect, for when the performance was over the judge called Eppie aside and asked, "Is that Foote boy afflicted or is that acting?" She assured them it was acting and they gave me first prize for best actor.

Eppie saw to it that I was cast in all the plays she did in my sophomore, junior and senior years, none of them memorable, but they kept me acting.

Where did all this start? I remember walking in summer evenings, with my parents and my brothers, the smell of honeysuckle everywhere, and we would often pass a small Victorian cottage, on whose porch a distinguished white-haired gentleman would be seated. He and my parents always exchanged greetings and once after we were a few yards away my father said, "That's Mr. Armstrong and he was in the cotton fields of Mississippi when he got a call to come to Texas and preach."

"What does that mean, Daddy?" I asked.

"What does what mean, Son?"

"Getting a call."

"He's a Baptist, Son," he said as if that explained everything.

"Is that why he got a call, because he's a Baptist?"

"Well, now . . ."

"Can only Baptists get a call?"

"No, honey," my mother ever patient said. "Methodists can, too, and Presbyterians and Episcopalians."

"What about Holy Rollers?" I asked.

"I expect they can, too, darling," Mother said. "I just don't happen to know any."

"Why do they call them Holy Rollers?" I asked.

"I don't know, precious. Do you, hon?" she asked my father.

"No, sweetheart, I don't; preachers have a hard life," he added as if to discourage any of his sons from the notion of getting that kind of call.

"Do Holy Rollers have preachers?" I continued asking.

"I wouldn't know, sweetheart. I'm sure they do," my mother said.

"Maybe they roll around, and that's why they are called Holy Rollers."

"Maybe so, honey."

When I was eleven, I got a call, so to speak, not to be a

preacher, but an actor. It came to me as clearly as I presume Mr. Armstrong's call came to him that acting was what I wanted to do. And I never wavered from that call either until I began writing, some ten years later, and the desire to act left me as suddenly as it had arrived.

Chapter 2

I was born Tuesday, March 14, 1916, in a rented room in the town of Wharton, Texas. The *Wharton Spectator,* founded by two of my great-uncles, printed the following item on Friday, March 18, 1916:

> Mr. and Mrs. Horton Foote were the proud parents of a son born Tuesday.

My mother, twenty-two, was Harriet Gautier Brooks, named for her paternal grandmother, but always called Hallie. My father, twenty-six, was Albert Horton Foote, named for his father and great-grandfather, and I was named Albert Horton Foote, Jr.

What the bland *Spectator* item gave no hint of was the conflict that preceded my birth.

My mother's parents, Daisy and Tom Brooks, strenuously opposed the marriage, forcing my mother and my father to elope. They didn't elope very far, just five blocks across town to the rented house of their friends Allie and Arch Elmore. They were married in the Elmores' parlor by the Baptist minister. The Methodist minister, whose parishioners included my mother's family, had refused to marry them, and the Baptist minister agreed only on the condition that my mother call her parents and tell them what she was about to do. Her mother wasn't at home, so she called her father at his office, ten minutes before the ceremony was to begin, and he pleaded with her not to marry, as he was certain she would regret it the rest of her life. She didn't take his advice and in the late afternoon, on Valentine's Day, 1915, with only a few friends present, my mother and father were married. It was a marriage that lasted almost sixty years. I was always fascinated how they could manage the secrecy of all this, given the smallness of Wharton, the town then less than three thousand, and where like most small towns, everyone knew everyone else, and I would often question them about how they managed the elopement without my mother's parents knowing about it.

"Well, Son," my father would explain, "I had some good friends here at the time."

"Who were your friends?" I asked.

"Well, Barsoty, and Felix and Robert Rockwood, Arch Elmore. I got Barsoty to go to the jewelry store to buy the wedding ring and he made like it was for buying it for a girl he knew, and then I went to El Campo for the marriage license."

"Why did you go to El Campo?" I asked.

"Because if I had gotten it here at the courthouse, where your mother's father and mother had a lot of friends, someone would march right over to Mr. Brooks's office to tell him and then he would try to stop it."

"Mother."

"Yes, Son."

"Were you nervous?"

"Yes."

"Were you scared?"

"Yes, honey, scared to death."

"What time of day did you get married?"

"Five o'clock," my father said.

"What time did you leave home for the wedding, Mother?"

"I didn't leave home for the wedding. I told Mama I was going to spend the day with Allie, and I'd slipped the dress I got married in over to Allie's the day before, and so Mama and Papa didn't suspect anything."

"Did your aunts know about it, Daddy?"

"Yes, they did."

"And did they approve?"

"Yessir."

"What about your mama?"

"Well, she was living in Houston, and I never saw much of Mama after she married Mr. Cleveland and moved to Houston."

"So she didn't know you were getting married?"

"Not until after. I wrote her a letter the week after the wedding."

"Was she happy about it?"

"I think so."

"We lived at Allie and Archie's house for three months after our marriage, you know," Mother said.

"No, I didn't know that," I said.

"And then we rented a room from Mrs. Grat Huston."

"That's when I was born, wasn't it?"

"That's right."

"Then we took our meals across the street at Mrs. Walker's boardinghouse."

"Why did you take your meals there?"

"Because we couldn't cook at Mrs. Huston's."

"Why?"

"Because we only had one room, and she didn't allow cooking."

"Did you like eating at the boardinghouse?"

"No," my father said. "I didn't."

"Now, hon, it was all right," my mother said.

"Wasn't Mrs. Walker a good cook?" I asked.

"Oh, she could cook all right," my father said. "But she never gave you enough. I always walked away hungry. After we were married Mr. and Mrs. Brooks wouldn't speak to us."

"Wouldn't speak to you?"

"No, sir. Not for a whole year."

"Did it make you sad, Mother?"

"Yes, it did."

"It was a mess, let me tell you," my father said. "My aunt Loula and my aunt Lida and my aunt Reenie stopped speaking then to the Brookses."

"Why?"

"Because they wouldn't speak to me and Mother."

"Wouldn't they speak to you even if you passed them uptown?"

"We never met uptown," my mother said. "Once I saw Mama in the distance walking down the street and she must have seen me because she suddenly turned around and went back in the other direction."

"When did they start speaking to you again?"

"Well, when they heard I was going to have a baby."

"That was me?"

"Yes."

"Who told them you were going to have a baby?"

"I don't know that, Son. All I know was that one day Bessie Marcus was visiting with me in my room at Mrs. Huston's . . ."

"Who is Bessie Marcus?"

"She was a little girl that lived down the street," my mother said. "She was a simple little thing, but sweet, and I was glad for her company. She used to call me Mary."

"Why did she call you that?"

"I never knew. One day I said to her, Bessie, my name is Hallie, not Mary. She looked at me for a minute, not acknowledging my correction at all, and the next day when she came to see me, she went right on calling me Mary."

"Didn't you say anything to her then?"

"No. I just gave up. Anyway, it was that day the phone rang at Mrs. Huston's and she answered it and came to my room and said it was for me, and as I went towards the phone, she said, Hallie, I think it's your mother."

"How did that make you feel?"

"Nervous. Anyway, I went to the phone pretending I didn't know who it was and I said, Hello, and Mama said, Hallie, it's your mama."

"And what did you say?"

"Well, I couldn't think of anything to say. I hadn't heard her voice in such a long time I was afraid I was going to cry, and so I just said, Hello, Mama, how are you? And she said, I'm fine, thank you. I thought I'd come over to see you this afternoon if you're going to be home. Yes, ma'm. I'm going to be here, I said. I'll be there around three, she said, and hung up."

"And did she come over?"

"Yes."

"And did she say she was sorry?"

"No, she just began talking like she had seen me the day before. The rift between us was never mentioned then and it has never been mentioned until this day."

"When did Papa come over?"

"The next day. Alone."

"Did he call first?"

"No. He just appeared, and he said he was going to build a house for us so we'd have a house to take the baby to."

"My goodness," I said.

The house was built in early 1917, its backyard adjoining the backyard of my grandparents. A sturdy, simple six-room cottage high off the ground, to protect it from frequent floods, with a front porch almost halfway around the house. I was brought there when I was just a year old, and I live there again now. It has seen few changes through the years, although everything around it has completely changed.

My parents were given three-quarters of an acre with the house, part of a fifteen-acre plot belonging to my grandfather. His house, barn and outbuildings were also on two of the acres; the rest were in pasture or used for growing cotton or corn, depending on the mood of Uncle Joe, a black man, who grew the crops. He also was the yardman and general hired man for my grandparents. I don't remember what arrangement he had with them about the corn or cotton acreage, but I suspect he was farming it on shares. Uncle Joe (I never knew his last name) was small, wiry and very dark. He called my grandmother "Old Missy" and my mother "Young Missy."

* * *

My grandfather's fifteen acres had originally been part of the William Kincheloe plantations. Kincheloe, who received title to two leagues of land from the Mexican government on July 8, 1824, was one of the original three hundred settlers that came to Texas from Louisiana with Stephen Austin. He chose for his two plantations the alluvial land adjacent to Caney Creek and the Colorado River. This land grew switch cane along the creek, dwarfing, it was said, man and beast, and giant native pecans and live oak trees dripping with Spanish moss.

The Kincheloe plantation had been divided and subdivided many times before my grandfather bought his acreage in 1896, which included a Victorian cottage of six rooms. Later, in the early twenties, the house was remodeled and enlarged by my grandparents into the handsome one that I remember.

The house was set well back from Richmond Road, which was graveled then; four live oak trees lined the road, on one side of the yard were three more live oaks and directly in front of the house to the right of the porch steps was the cypress tree. On the opposite side of the yard was a huge sycamore tree and, beyond that, close to the side of the house were three fig trees. In the backyard were a pecan, a persimmon and a pomegranate tree.

The house was built high off the ground, so high, in fact, that I could and did play underneath it as a child, walking about very comfortably until I was ten or so. The porch or gallery was twelve feet wide, and here was a swing and comfortable wicker rocker chairs (five as I remember). A great deal of time, especially at night or early morning, was spent on the porch by the family.

Inside, the house was divided by a hall, wide enough for a good-size Oriental rug, a grandfather clock, and a table against the right wall. On the left, as you entered the hall, was the living room, high ceilinged, with three tall windows on the street side of the room, and two higher windows on either side of the fireplace, rarely used in our mild climate. In the living room were a Victrola and a baby grand piano. I remember my aunt Laura singing to the family here, my mother accompanying her on the piano. Their rendition of "Sweet Alice Ben Bolt" always moved me to tears, which caused my aunt to point out that I was very "tender-hearted."

The dining room adjoined the living room, separated by glass sliding doors, and behind it were a breakfast room and a kitchen. On the other side of the house was my grandparents' bedroom, an enormous room furnished with a huge Victorian bed, wardrobe, bureau, chaise longue and several rocking chairs. There were more bedrooms, big too, one of them leading on to a sun parlor, as large as the living room. The sun parlor had windows all around.

Besides being tender-hearted, I also must have had an active imagination. Until the age of five, when I was enrolled in the first grade, I had been restricted to playing with my friends either in my yard, my grandparents' yard, or the Wilsons' yard across the street from my grandparents. But I had made friends at school with Lindsay Carter, who lived in an old plantation house, long since torn down, near the livery stable, also long gone, on the now drained Caney Creek. To get there I had to walk for several blocks down a dirt road surrounded by cotton fields. Once on the way back home through the cotton fields, I began to run as fast as I could, for no apparent reason that I can remember, and by the time I got to my house I was out of breath and covered with the dust of the road. I ran to my mother and in panic told her that as I was coming through the cotton fields a mad dog started toward me, growling and foaming at the mouth. Just when it had almost reached me, Mr. Pitman, the town marshal, had come along on his spotted pony, reached down and grabbed me in the nick of time, shot the mad dog and so saved my life. My mother swallowed my story hook, line and sinker and when my father came home that night she told him of the miracle that had saved me from being bitten by a mad dog. My father equally gullible grabbed me and hugged me and said, "I always did like old Pit." The next morning on his way to the store he met Mr. Pitman and he ran up to him, extending his hand, and said, "Pit, I want to thank you for saving my boy's life." When Pitman looked blank and replied, "How is that, Al?" my father said he knew he and my mother had been taken. I was not punished for my fancy; instead it became a family tale illustrating my imaginative power and their gullibility.

I've often heard my mother and her sisters wonder how they all managed to fit into the original house of my grandparents. Besides their six children, my grandmother and grandfather's household included at one time or other my grandmother's parents, her brother, my grandfather's nephew and during the hurricane season assorted aunts and cousins from the Gulf Coast. When the relatives were gone, they often housed Mrs. Page, an elderly impoverished lady who had been married to a Methodist minister. At night her snoring kept the rest of the house awake.

My grandparents were always generous to the poor and needy, black and white. There was one white family called the Campbells that my grandmother took a special interest in. She regularly invited Mrs. Campbell and her spinster sister, Miss Mag, for meals, and often took them for afternoon rides in her buggy. Mrs. Campbell was plump, with abundant gray hair, and the Methodist Ladies would dress her up as Martha Washington and use her to pour tea for their annual Washington's Birthday tea. Mrs. Campbell and Miss Mag shared their run-down house with Mrs. Campbell's son, his wife and their many children. The son died and my grandparents offered to host the Campbells and their friends after the funeral. My grandparents supplied an abundance of food, more food than I suspect the Campbells had seen in many a day. They and their friends and neighbors stayed on and on. When it was time finally to say their good-byes, Miss Mag was the last to express her appreciation and she said to my grandfather, as she took his hand, "Mr. Tom, I want to thank you for the most enjoyable day of my life."

The three-quarter acre given to my parents was treeless, except for a chinaberry tree in the backyard, and one of the first things my father did was to plant two pecan trees in our front yard, and two fig trees in the back. My father also fenced in the backyard and built a chicken house. The instant he got home from his store at night he would change his clothes and go out to tend the chickens. As a small boy I was given one of the baby chickens as a pet. It was kept on the back porch and I was devoted to it. It would follow me around like a puppy and I played with it for hours on end. After a week, though, the poor little thing died. I was heartbroken and my mother and father were very sympathetic and helped me plan a proper funeral.

I was never allowed to have a dog, because of the chickens, but I had a number of cats. Later, when I was twelve and my father had given up the chickens and started a garden, my uncle Brother (my mother's oldest brother) gave me a horse for Christmas. We used the former chicken house as a barn, because my grandfather's barn had long since been torn down and a garage for cars was in its place. I named my horse Minnie after Minnie the Moocher in Cab Calloway's song. I rode Minnie every day, and as no one had told me anything about caring for a horse, after I would run her as fast as I could, I would immediately give her all the water she wanted to drink. When I left home at sixteen, Minnie was sent out to a friend's farm. It seemed my running her and letting her drink water immediately afterward had crippled her in some way and in the unsentimental tradition of farmers they had her killed.

Chapter 3

The Ku Klux Klan was a real political force in Texas during my childhood. I remember being held by my grandfather—my mother, father, grandmother, aunts and uncles all beside us—as we stood on the wide front gallery of their house to watch at night as the Klan, carrying torches, marched down Richmond Road from the old schoolhouse, on their way to the Courthouse Square. And one rainy afternoon (I must have been five), I remember rummaging through some bottom kitchen cabinets while my mother was fixing supper, and finding a Ku Klux Klan robe.

"Mother?"

"Yes, Son?"

"What's this?" I said, holding up the robe.

"Give me that," she said, and I could tell she was very upset.

"I don't know why your daddy didn't burn this. Where did you find it?"

"Under here in the cabinet. What is it, Mother?"

"It's a Ku Klux Klan robe."

"Where did Daddy get it?"

"Oh, Lord. There are a lot of members of the Klan here and he and Papa got pressured to go to one of their meetings, and they went together."

"Does Papa have a robe, too?"

"Yes, unless he's gotten rid of it. I hope he has. Anyway, both Papa and your daddy were disgusted by what they saw and heard."

"Why were they disgusted?"

"Because they didn't agree with what was being said or who was saying it."

"What was being said?"

"Lord, honey. Just a lot of foolishness. Anyway, they were so disgusted they never went back."

My father, a lifelong and passionate Democrat, indeed a yellow-dog Democrat, had no use for the Klan or any of their candidates. They were, of course, violently anti-Catholic, anti-Semitic and anti-black. In 1928, at the National Democratic Convention in Houston, Al Smith was nominated for president. My father and mother, who were great Smith supporters, went for a day to the convention. The Democratic party for years had been the only party in our town and the nomination of Smith (a Catholic) caused great division and bitterness among many of their friends.

The night of the election—we had a radio by then—my uncle Brother, also a rabid Democrat, came over to listen to the returns with my parents.

My mother fixed an early supper and everyone sat in the living room with paper and sharpened pencils to write down the results as they came in.

"Oh, I tell you I have a good feeling," my father said. "That Al Smith is going to win."

"I bet ten dollars today he would," Uncle Brother said.

"Are you excited, hon?" my father asked my mother.

"Yes, I am."

"Sister, do you think he's going to win?" Uncle Brother asked.

"I certainly hope so," Mother said.

"I tell you the day we visited the Democratic Convention in Houston was one of the greatest days of my life," my father said.

"Why do people hate him so here?" my uncle Brother said. "Because he's a Catholic?"

"That's it. They come in the store all the time, and say, do you mean you're going to vote for that Catholic? And I tell them you bet your boots I am."

The early returns were not promising, and my uncle Brother looked worried, but my father kept on being cheerful.

"That's just the early returns," he said. "They mean nothing at all. Wait until New York comes in."

"What about Texas?" I asked.

"God knows what Texas will do, Son," my father said. "The Baptists run Texas, but they don't run me."

But as the returns continued to give him no comfort, as it looked increasingly like Hoover was going to win by a landslide, my father's enthusiasm and hope turned to depression and gloom. Finally, when it was apparent that Al Smith had been badly beaten, the radio was turned off and the pencils put away. My father was depressed for weeks.

Later I heard with pride that Professor Autrey, the school superintendent, had prayed over whom to vote for president, and it came to him that my grandfather Mr. Tom Brooks (who was dead by then), a man he admired very much, would have voted for Al Smith, Catholic or not. That's what he did.

* * *

Henry Schulze was always a living reminder of the Klan to me. He was a morose, dark-complected man, and I would see him wandering around town or sitting alone on the porch of his house. The rumor had spread that he was living with a black woman who had been hired to look after his senile mother. The Klan supposedly sent him warnings to break off the relationship, but he ignored them, and one day he was seized by a group of the Klan, tarred and feathered and turned loose in front of Outlar's Drugstore. He lived many years after, always alone. I never saw him talking to anyone. And what happened to him was told over and over long after the Klan in our town had been abandoned.

After all these years a recounting of what happened was reprinted in the "Seventy-five Years Ago" column in our local paper. It read:

TAR AND FEATHERING
June 24, 1921

Wharton man is kidnapped, tarred and feathered in broad daylight! Henry Schulze was stopped at Richmond and Milam by masked men about 3 p.m. while riding his horse. The men, at gun point, ordered him into their car. Later Schulze was dumped on the corner of Milam and Houston, minus his clothes, having been whipped, his hair cut off, tarred and feathered. He stated he recognized no one and harbored no malice for the deed and was totally innocent of the conduct his assailants accused him of.

The Klan was only one form of an extremely primitive social order in Wharton and Wharton County, where, as in a great deal of Texas, only whites could vote in local and state elections. A White Man's Union had been started in 1889, in protest against what the whites claimed was the domination of Republican Northern carpetbaggers, who they claimed were using the majority Negro population to control all elections.

Only white men could belong to the White Man's Union, and the only candidates allowed on the voting ballots were those nominated by the union. The nominees also had to be registered Democrats—Republicans were completely shut out and this continued until the passing of Lyndon Johnson's Voting Rights Act in 1965.

By the time I was growing up all this was just a memory. The handful of white Republicans left joined the White Man's Union, so they could vote in local and state elections. The blacks were totally disenfranchised from voting except in national elections, and even then had to pay a poll tax, which few of them could afford.

I took all of this for granted, if I wondered about it at all, as I accepted all the evils of segregation: separate schools, drinking fountains, toilets, blacks being banned from white restaurants and the soda fountains in white drugstores. Lynching of blacks had mostly ended by 1914, but once in a while one lynching or another would be recalled to define a certain period of time in Wharton or Wharton County. I don't remember anyone saying how terrible they were, or seeming glad they had ended. The tales were told with no apparent moral concerns.

My cousin Nannie Bennett from Angleton, Texas, the granddaughter of my great-aunt Nannie Stafford, was once inadvertently involved in a lynching. She was twenty-three when she first told me the story, and she repeated it many times through the years as I'm sure it was troubling to her.

"What do you mean you were involved in a lynching, Nannie?" I asked that first time.

"Well, you know the Mastersons in Angleton?"

"Are we kin to them?"

"No," she said. "We are kin to Jo Masterson, who was a Smith. We are kin to the Smiths. They all came to Texas from Virginia together."

"Who did?"

"The Brookses and the Smiths."

"Oh. What do the Mastersons have to do with a lynching?"

"Well, when I was a little girl . . ."

"What do you mean a little girl?"

"I was a little girl, that's what I mean. I was five. Anyway, I was playing with a friend in the Mastersons' backyard and I cut my foot and got blood in the backyard. I went home then to get it bandaged and then came back to play some more. The Mastersons had a black trustee from the prison farm working for them, and that same day a white woman from the North was found raped and murdered, and the black trustee was suspected of the crime and arrested. The Mastersons felt he was innocent and defended him, but blood was found in the yard of the Mastersons' house and in the kitchen. They had a trial and the Negro convict . . ."

"What was his name?"

"The convict's?"

"Yes."

"Leroy, something or other. And he said the blood in the yard came from my cut, and the blood in the kitchen came from my cut, too. Well, my daddy asked me if I had gone into the kitchen and I said no, I hadn't."

"Hadn't you gone into the kitchen?"

"No. I went home after I cut my foot. Anyway, my daddy told the prosecuting attorney what I had said, and the prosecuting attorney asked me if I had gone into the kitchen, and I said no, I hadn't, and he said, are you sure, and I said, yessir, I was sure, and he put me on the stand and he asked me again if I had gone into the Mastersons' kitchen and I said, no, sir, and he said, are you real sure, and I said, yessir, I am, and the judge believed me and convicted the Negro convict. That night another Negro man in the same jail cell asked to speak to the sheriff privately, and told the sheriff that Leroy, or whatever his name was, said that if he ever got out of jail, he would kill that little white girl that had said she hadn't gone into the kitchen of the Masterson house. His threat got out around town, and when my daddy heard it, he organized a posse and they went to the jail and made the sheriff turn over the Negro convict to them. They took him outside to the jail yard and hung him. And a picture of that man hanging from a tree in the jail yard was kept in our kitchen, and whenever a Negro man or woman came to work for us, it was shown to them and my daddy would say, this is what happens to Negroes who get out of line in Angleton."

Many years later when I got to know my cousin Peter Masterson in New York, we discussed all this and he said his family still felt that the trustee was innocent and a great injustice had been done.

Chapter 4

I was the fourth generation of Hortons to be born in Wharton. My great-great-grandfather Albert Clinton Horton had come to Texas from Alabama with his wife, Eliza Holliday, in 1834, settling on the Gulf Coast in Matagorda County. The following year he returned to Alabama to recruit volunteers known as the Mobile Grays to join Texas in her fight for independence. He served in the Texas Army from February to May 1836. He represented Matagorda, Jackson and Victoria counties in the First and Second Texas Congress from 1836 to 1838. After Texas was admitted into the Union in 1845, he was elected lieutenant governor and served as governor from May 1846 until July 1847 during the absence of Governor J. Pinckney Henderson, who was commander of the Texas troops during the Mexican War.

Sometime in the early 1840s, Horton bought another plantation on the upper part of Matagorda County in what is now Wharton County. He built a large two-story house on his land, calling it Sycamore Grove. The plantation house served six generations before it was torn down in 1960.

I saw the house only twice, once when I was a young man and

my cousin Lida Croom Hodges, who lived in the house with her husband, invited me to a dinner party. The house had been built by slaves from trees on the plantation, and I remember few architectural details inside or out except that I was impressed by the size of the dining room and the width of the floorboards. I was also impressed by the china and silver, as I had been told by my great-aunt Loula to pay attention to it, because, she said bitterly, and with great authority, my branch of the family should have had a share of all that. I rode out to the plantation many years later with my wife and children. We didn't go inside the house, but stayed in the yard. My cousin was still living there and she said to my son, who was named after me, that it was nice to have two Albert Hortons again on the plantation.

Governor Horton and Eliza Holliday had six children. All, except Patience Louisiana Texas, the oldest, and Robert John, the youngest, and my great-grandfather, died during an outbreak of yellow fever.

Patience was married at twenty-one to Colonel I. N. Dennis, and died in 1863. They had one child, Lida Horton Dennis. Sometime before Patience's death her father had deeded the plantation, the plantation house and half of his 170 slaves to her, and at her death she left everything to her daughter.

Robert Horton, my great-grandfather, was in the Confederate Army at the time of his sister's and father's death. When he returned to Sycamore Grove after the war he learned that it now belonged to his niece and was managed by her father, Colonel Dennis. In his father's will Robert had been left half of the slaves, but they were all freed by then.

Robert Horton married Mary Hawes in 1866. Mary Hawes was the daughter of Hugh Walker Hawes, who had sold his plantation in Kentucky and had come to Texas in 1853, and bought an island in the gulf called Saluria hoping to make it a port to rival Galveston.

Robert and Mary Horton had six children: Corrella (called Corrie), Louisiana Texas Patience (called Loula), Mary, Albert Clinton, Reenie and Lida. Robert took his family to Saluria Island where he was employed managing the lighthouse. He was on duty there when a fierce gulf hurricane followed by a tidal wave swept the island. His family, alone in their house at the other end of the island, was forced to climb to the roof to escape drowning. He took them away soon after to live in Goliad, and a few years later to Wharton.

Albert Harrison Foote, a young lawyer, had come to Wharton some years before with his widowed mother and five brothers and sisters. The Footes had originally come from Virginia in the early 1850s to Galveston where their father bought and sold cotton. They, too, were bankrupt at the close of the war.

Corrella Horton and Albert Harrison Foote were married in Wharton on August 31, 1889. They had two children; the older was my father and the younger a girl they named Lily Dale. The marriage was not a happy one. According to my grandmother Corrella, my grandfather's brothers and sisters were never industrious, and Albert became the sole support of his family. He began to drink excessively and when the children were still quite young she left him and moved back into her parents' home. Later, Corrella went to Houston to work as a seamstress at Munn's department store, taking Lily Dale with her and leaving my father to live in Wharton with his Horton grandparents.

My father told me little about his own father. I have only seen one picture of him, faded and stained, and I don't know if he was tall or thin, brunet or blond. He did tell me once that the day of his father's funeral (he was ten), a friend of his father's held him on his lap and told him what a fine man his father was and what a brilliant lawyer.

Many years later Mrs. Hall, a friend of our family's gave me some books (including works of Thackeray and Bulwer-Lytton) that she said had belonged to my grandfather Foote. When my father saw them he said, "I know where she got them. From her husband, who was a saloonkeeper, and I'm sure my father gave them to him to pay a whiskey debt."

My mother told me how it always bothered my father that when his father died, the family was so poor they couldn't afford a tombstone for his grave. The first money he was able to save after they married he used to buy one.

Wharton, when my father was a boy in the 1890s, had a population of less than a thousand. The town was bordered on the south by the Colorado River and on the north by Caney Creek. Rainfall was heavy and the river and the creek often flooded. There were no stock laws and livestock of all kinds were free to roam the town.

I have been told that often there was so much mud in the streets around the square that it took four mules to pull a wagon, and the mud was so thick you couldn't see the wheels.

In the stagnant water of Caney Creek, a block from the center of town, dead dogs, cats, chickens and fish floated. In the summer when the creek was low, it was covered by a thick scum under which the fish died by the thousands, and men would gather them up in wagons and carry them away. Buzzards sat on the creek banks and devoured the fish. Wharton then had a particularly virulent form of malaria, known as black jaundice, as well as typhoid and yellow fever. The common remedy for all afflictions was calomel and quinine, still the common remedy for most illness when I was growing up.

As a boy I often tried to imagine the Wharton that my great-great-grandfather Albert Clinton Horton knew, the Wharton that Robert Horton returned to, the Wharton that my father had grown up in.

Mrs. Sallie Stewart Gallahar, who claimed to be the first white child born in Wharton, in 1836, and still alive when I was a boy, said that there were only a few houses then, some of logs, some of lumber and some of brick made by slave labor. On the outskirts were plantations, including the Horton plantation.

For many years Wharton remained a village with no sidewalks and no streets and no proper drainage of creeks and sanitation. Practically all the buildings were wooden and faced the square. Fires occurred frequently and the worst fire happened in 1902, which nearly wiped out the west side of the square.

It had more saloons at the time than any other businesses and nice ladies did not walk on the side of the square where the saloons were located.

The Wharton my mother and father knew boasted several blocks of brick buildings, but the streets were neither paved nor graveled. There were houses interspersed between the stores, each having a substantial yard, and many of these houses were still standing when I was a boy. The Robert Horton house, a large, rambling, white two-story structure, had been one of them, but it was torn down soon after his death in 1914.

The Horton plantation was now in possession of Patience's great-grandsons: Wylie and Franklin Hodges.

To outsiders, there seemed to be no resentment between the two branches of the family, Patience's branch living on the plantation, Robert's branch eking out some kind of living in Wharton. But inside Robert's family, the Horton girls, as they were always called, continued to keep alive the injustice they felt had been done to their father.

It was their version I was raised on, particularly the one often told me by my great-aunt Loula.

I was twelve when I knew Loula best. She was a tall regal woman in her sixties. She had dyed black hair and was partial to the color red, using it in her house and dress as often as possible. A born storyteller, she introduced me into our family habit of constant speculation about the past, its meaning and its consequences.

Her repertory was large and varied. It included the dances (she always called them balls) she attended as a girl at the opera house; her beaux before she married her husband; the slights done her or her sisters; the day the whole family had been read out of the Baptist Church for dancing and card playing, causing them to join the Episcopal Church; the ghost she called the lady in white, who appeared often at night in her house, always combing long blond hair. And then she would return, with greater and greater vigor, to her version of how her father had been cheated of his birthright.

"Auntie, tell me again about Philips," I'd say, and she'd be off.

She would begin by closing her eyes, and shaking her head solemnly. Then pointing in the direction of the Horton plantation, with a slight sneer on her lips and a superior look on her face, as if to let you know that though nothing could be proved, she knew only too well the truth of what had gone on, she would slowly and dramatically begin to unfold a Machiavellian plot of intrigue and treachery perpetrated by Colonel Dennis to cheat her father, then hardly more than a boy, and off in the Confederate Army fighting for the South.

"But, Sonny," she would say, her face clouded with anger, "don't you ever forget this and don't let your children ever forget it, the chief villain was Philips."

"He was adopted by Governor Horton, wasn't he?"

"I guess he was," she sighed.

"How did that happen?" I asked for the hundredth time, and she answered as if I had never asked the question before.

"When my father, your great-grandfather, was ten or so, his father worried that he could not get a proper education in Texas and sent him to school in the East."

"Where in the East?"

"I don't remember, darling, but he was teased in the school by the other boys."

"Why?"

"Because he arrived wearing his hair in a queue and became violently homesick. You know what a queue is, darling?"

"No."

"Well, a long time ago men had long hair and they would take the ends of it and make what we call a ponytail now."

"Oh."

She kept her eyes closed now as she talked as if she were in great pain.

"So his father decided to bring him home. For the return trip they took a boat from New York to Matagorda, and on their way to the boat, they met on the dock a young bootblack who had been orphaned. Governor Horton, worrying that on the plantation his son would have no white companions to play with, decided to adopt the boy and bring him to Texas as a companion for my father."

"And this was Philips?"

"Yes, God help us. This was Philips."

"That bootblack," she continued, speaking the word *bootblack* with scorn and derision, "six years older than my blessed father, was raised in the plantation house," she would say, pointing in the direction of the plantation. "And, of course, he was given every privilege given to my father. He was educated as a lawyer."

"Why was he educated as a lawyer?"

"In the hopes, I suppose, that he would always protect and advise my father, still a young boy, in the event of Governor Horton's death. Instead after Governor Horton died of a broken heart . . ."

"How do you know he died of a broken heart, Auntie?" I asked, already knowing her answer.

"Because of the collapse of the Confederacy. He lost everything. He had all his money in Confederate currency and bonds and they were worthless. The slaves were freed and everything was in chaos. Total chaos, and that skunk . . ." She paused then to catch her breath. "Philips teamed with you know who."

"Who?" I asked, pleading ignorance.

"Dennis, and together they robbed my father of everything. Everything. Everything, and don't you ever forget it."

"No, ma'm."

"And don't you ever, ever forget it," she repeated again with great force.

So forceful and dramatic was her telling of this story that as a boy I was filled with a desire for revenge on all concerned, especially Philips.

It was puzzling to me that after such tales of betrayal and deceit I would see her greet and embrace the very descendants of these perpetrators, when they met on the street, and affectionately call them cousin.

My father, usually practical and unsentimental about the past, told me he agreed with Aunt Loula's version of the events, but warned me against dwelling on it as it did no good.

I was puzzled why Robert Horton had done nothing to expose the injustice done to him. "What could he do, Son," my father would patiently explain. "You have to realize how things were in those days. It was Reconstruction. The carpetbaggers and Yankees controlled everything. Legal records at the courthouse were destroyed or disappeared mysteriously. He tried as best he could, but he was helpless."

I wonder now what really happened in that long-ago time. I am friendly now with all my cousins still living and descending from Patience. One of them, Lida Croom Hodges Mills, was as puzzled as I had been by Robert's disinheritance. She had a copy of his father's will, which she gave me to read. It was drawn up when Robert was twelve and Patience was married to Colonel Dennis. The only mention of Robert in the will was that he was to be given half the slaves.

Five years ago, I mentioned Mr. Philips to Lida. She had never heard of him. I then asked Thomas Abell, another cousin, descendant of Robert Horton, and a lawyer, about Philips and he had never heard of him either. Did Philips ever exist? I'll never know now, because my father, my great-aunt Loula or anyone else who might know the truth about his existence are long since dead.

Thomas Abell is dead now, too, but before his death he studied the will that Lida Croom had given me and concluded that Robert had been cheated. He promised to show me (using the will) how he had come to his conclusion, but he died before he had the chance.

Through the years the Horton plantation was sold off piece by piece by Patience's heirs. Its cotton and cane fields are now overrun with housing developments and all that's left of Sycamore Grove are six magnificent sycamore trees, at least one hundred and fifty years old, and a small family graveyard. The only mention of a Horton is a plaque on the iron fence surrounding the graves that reads:

Erected in 1925 by W.J. Croom in loving memory of his mother-in-law Mrs. P.L.T. Dennis, wife of Col. I.N. Dennis, their two infant sons, Gov. A.C. Horton's mother and Mrs. Sadie Dennis.

Chapter 5

My father lived on with his grandparents in Wharton and went to school there through the sixth grade. He worked around town after school doing anything to make a few dollars. He sold fish he caught in the river and empty whiskey bottles he found in the alleys back of the saloons and whorehouses. At twelve he left Wharton to work with his uncle Albert in a plantation store about ten miles downriver from Wharton. After a few months Albert left, restless for town and his gambling friends, leaving my father in charge of the store. My father lived with Martha and Douglas, a black couple, while he worked at the plantation store and he often told me it was one of the happiest times of his life. At Christmas his aunts and grandparents sent word for him to come home for the day but he refused, preferring to spend it with his black friends. He always insisted, however, that though he loved his grandparents and his aunts, the plantation was where he was happiest. He was no hunter—indeed, he never owned a gun or allowed me or my brothers to own one—but he loved to fish and wander through the plantation woods and fields.

His grandparents had little money, but there was great love

and affection in the family and my father always insisted he felt welcomed in that affection. The five sisters adored their parents and each other, and though they worried about their brother, Albert, and his by now obsessive interest in gambling, they were loyal and steadfast in their devotion to him too.

Four of the girls played musical instruments, all self-taught. Loula, the banjo and the piano; Mary, the violin; Reenie, the guitar; and Lida, the ukelele, and every night they would entertain their young friends with their music. They sang, too, my father remembering particularly their versions of "Dixie" and "Beautiful Dreamer." They all loved to dance and had many beaux. Loula, whom my father loved best of all, was the plainest, yet the most popular, he said, because of her charm and personality.

I loved hearing Aunt Loula tell of the days when she and her sisters were still living at home, not yet married. I would get her started by asking her to play one of the old songs, and she would look at me for a second as if trying to decide if she could still remember it.

"I play by ear, you know," she would say. "I can't tell one note from another," but then inevitably she would go to the piano and play "Beautiful Dreamer" or "Dark Town Strutter's Ball."

"Isn't that 'Dark Town Strutter's Ball,' Auntie?" I would ask.

"Yes, Sonny," she would reply.

"And didn't they play that the night you led the cakewalk at the ball at the opera house?"

"Yes, they did."

"Who was your date that night?"

She would smile slyly then, trying to remember.

"My God, I had so many of them. Now, let's see," now again smiling, shaking her head, slowly thinking.

"Honey, I swear I can't remember. Maybe John Barton."

"John Barton?"

"Yes, John Barton."

"I never knew him."

"No, you wouldn't. He was dead before you were born. He was drowned in the river. A group of young people went on a boat ride one moonlight night, and John Barton decided to go for a swim and he dived off the side of the boat . . ."

"With all his clothes on?"

"Yes, all except his shoes. He was a daredevil, you know, and a suck hole grabbed him and right before our eyes pulled him under. Took them a week to find the body. You could hear them dynamiting down at the river day and night trying to recover his body. The whole town mourned for him. They asked me and my sisters to sing at his funeral, but I was so overcome I couldn't, so Reenie, Lida and Mary had to sing without me."

"Why didn't my grandmother sing with you?"

"Oh, she was married to your grandfather by then. She had your daddy and your aunt Lily to take care of."

"If John Barton had lived would you have married him?"

"Oh, I don't know, darling, I had so many beaux in those days. Pinkney Rowe, Douglas Sorrel, Frank May, Buddy Curtis. I almost married one of them too."

"Which one?"

"I can't tell you that, darling. But I'll tell you something else, Papa took me aside and said, Loula, I have to tell you this. That young man you're planning to marry has outside children. Oh, heavens, Papa, I said, don't tell me that. I hate to tell you, honey, because I know you're fond of him, but it's true."

"Was it?"

"Yes, I'm sorry to say. He had three outside children."

"Three?"

"Three." Then she paused and started laughing, and turned to me and said, "Do you know why I'm laughing?"

"No. I have no idea."

"I'm just thinking of all the foolish things those beaux of mine said to me to win my affection." Then she paused, cocked her head to one side, closed her eyes and said solemnly, "Then Doc came along and when God made Doc he threw the pattern away."

"Was it love at first sight when you saw Uncle Doc?"

"Yes, Sonny, it was love at first sight, and let me tell you he is a saint."

After I left my aunt Loula's house the afternoon I first heard that story I went by my father's store. He was alone in the store.

"Daddy."

"Yes, Son."

"I've just visited Aunt Loula and she told me she was about to marry a man when her father told her he had outside children and she shouldn't marry him and she didn't. She wouldn't tell me his name. Do you know who it is?"

"Yes."

"Who is it?"

"I can't tell you that, Son."

"What does having outside children mean?"

"Children from out of wedlock and in this case black."

"Do I know him?"

"Yes, you see him in town every day of your life."

The Horton women, according to my mother, all had a terrible dread of childbirth. My other aunts never discussed the subject with me, but my great-aunt Loula often described its terror in vivid and graphic detail, always ending with: "Doc said they could tie him to the back of a wagon and drag him around the Courthouse Square before he would ever put me through that again."

"Doc" was Dr. John Irving, a dentist. Kind and soft-spoken, he was devoted to his wife. He would sit patiently for hours listening to her tales. He called her Kate, for whatever reason I never knew. He was our family dentist, and my mother often imitated his deadpan manner with his patients. After greeting them there was silence except for the command "Open," and then, after looking, it seemed to her, an eternity in one's mouth, came another command, "Close." Both "Open" and "Close" were invariably pronounced with the same solemnity. Doc and Loula had one child, Mary, whom they spoiled terribly.

Mary worshiped her quiet, patient father, but was often irritable with her mother, rolling her eyes with exasperation when Loula began one of her stories. I couldn't understand her hostility at all, particularly since I found the stories so fascinating.

One of my favorites was my aunt's account of the Saluria Island hurricane and tidal wave.

I knew how to get her started talking on that one too; all I had to do was casually ask her how old she was at the time of the hurricane on Saluria Island. She would listen to my question, think a moment and then her whole body would begin to tremble. The first time I saw her do that I became alarmed, and I said, "Are you all right, Auntie?"

"Yes, I'm all right," she said. "It's just that the memory of the horror of that night is always upsetting to me."

"Well, let's don't talk about it, if it upsets you, Auntie."

"No, I can talk about it," she insisted. "I'd like you to know what your family went through."

"Oh, I know storms can be terrible," I said.

"Oh, indeed," and then she gave a sarcastic laugh. "People here know nothing about storms. Now the nineteen hundred storm in Galveston was a storm, and the one we lived through in Saluria Island was a storm. Papa said he almost went crazy worrying about us. Oh, the house was shaking and the rain coming down in torrents, and Mama was alone with her children."

"How many of you were born then?"

"There were four of us. Corrie, Mary, Reenie and me."

"How old were you?"

"Ten. Corrie was twelve, Mary was eleven and Reenie was eight. At one time the wind was so fierce we thought the house would be torn apart. I was crying, and Mary was crying, and Corrie and Reenie were crying. And I kept saying, oh, if Papa were here, if Papa were only here, but of course he wasn't. He was in the lighthouse at the other end of the island." She closed her eyes then, shaking her head before continuing.

"Mama said, children, kneel down and pray, and I knelt down with the others, but I was crying so hard and I was so scared with the wind moaning and howling outside that I couldn't for the life of me pray, and all I could think to say was, Now I lay me down to sleep, I pray the Lord my soul to keep, if I should die before I wake. Well I got to that line about dying I began to cry even harder, and while I was crying and trying to pray the wind began to die down and Mama said our prayers are being answered, thank God, keep on praying children and so we all stayed on our knees and I tried again to pray, when I heard Sis scream . . . I opened my eyes and saw water coming in under the door, and I said, my God, Mama, we're going to all be drowned."

"Where was the water coming from?"

I knew very well of course. I had by this time heard the story many times.

"From the gulf. We didn't know it at the time, but a tidal wave was covering the island. Papa said later when he saw the tidal wave beginning, he prayed and he said, oh God, spare my wife and children. Anyway, the water was coming in fast by now and Mama said, girls if we stay in the house, we'll be caught like rats in a trap and we'll all be drowned. There is only one thing for us to do. Get on the roof of the house and pray the wind doesn't blow us away into the water, and that the water stops rising before it reaches the roof of our house. The water was coming in strong now. It was up to my waist and Mama said, come on children we've got to get to the roof and we went up the stairs to the attic and Mama opened the attic window and she said, now girls you have to get out the window and pull yourself up on the roof. Now I'm going first, and once I get up there I'll hold out my hand and help you. What if I fall Mama into the water, I said. I won't let you fall. Now, Reenie you'll go first since you're the youngest, and then Loula, she said, and then Mary and then Corrie." She would always pause then as if she were seeing it all again. "Mary is dead you know. She had TB and went out to West Texas with her husband where we all thought the climate would help her. But it did no good, she died out there. You know every once in a while there's this ghost appears in here. She has long blond hair and she just stands there combing it. I think it's my sister Mary. She had long blond hair you know, and has appeared to each generation. I bet she is going to appear to you one day, Sonny. The first time I saw her I was talking on the telephone to your mother and I fainted dead away. Doc, you know, never believed anyone had ever seen her. He just thought we had all imagined it. And then one night I woke up and Doc was sitting up in bed and I said what is it, Doc, and he said just be quiet, Loula, and I looked up then and there she was combing her hair and not saying a word."

"Did you ever try talking to her?"

"Yes, but she'd never answer. She would just disappear all of a sudden. I went to a fortune-teller once about it, and she said she was trying to tell us something about money. Either there was money buried under our house, or there was oil there. Mercy. Mercy. Mary has been dead such a long time now. Where was I, honey?"

"You were about to get up on the roof."

"Oh, yes. We all got up there someway. The wind had died down, thank God, but the rain was still coming in torrents and we were all huddled together, soaking wet, and then daylight came and the water kept rising higher and higher and was almost reaching the roof, when in the distance we saw a boat and Papa and some men were in the boat, and we all began to cry when we saw him and Papa and the men helped us off the roof and into the boat and took us back to the lighthouse and Papa said when we're all safe I'm taking you off this island and he did and we lived in Goliad for a while and Grandmother Horton came to live with us and then we moved back to Wharton."

"And you've been here ever since?" I said.

"Yes, we've been here ever since except for Mary who's buried out in West Texas."

"Why wasn't she buried here?"

"Papa didn't have the money to bring her body back here. We were all so poor then."

Another favorite of her stories was her version of the life and times of Miss Minnie May, a prototype of all such tales about the mystery of the town beauty becoming the town eccentric.

Miss Minnie May, as she was always referred to by my aunt, lived in a ramshackle one-story cottage, with a yard full of weeds, and judging from the sound as you passed, a lot of yapping dogs. Her husband, Bosie, never in my lifetime known to work, spent his days and most of the nights until the place closed sitting on a stool in Rugeley's drugstore, cigarette hanging out of his mouth. I would get my aunt talking about Miss Minnie by asking casually, as if I hadn't already heard it many times before, what was Miss Minnie like as a girl? She slowly shook her head from side to side as if trying to think of an adequate way to describe her to me, and after a few minutes, began:

"Well, first of all, darling, she was a beauty, to tell you the truth, she was the most beautiful girl I've ever known."

"The most beautiful, Auntie?"

"The most beautiful, and the sweetest, she was an angel, beloved by everyone, boys and girls, and her grace as a dancer was something the like of which I've never seen before or since."

"Was she popular with the young men?"

"She could have had her pick of them all, and she had an exquisite taste in clothes. I can see her now in a green riding dress she wore, green velvet it was, beautifully tailored. Oh, I can see her now in that green riding dress, riding through town on her horse at breakneck speed. Every single man in town wanted to marry her."

"Auntie?"

"Yes, Sonny."

"How old was she then?"

"Let's see. She was born in eighteen seventy and I'm talking now what eighteen eighty-six or -seven, so she would be seventeen, honey."

She sighed and then there was silence. I watched her.

"Auntie?"

"Yes?"

"Why did she marry Bosie?"

Again there was silence, another sigh, another shake of her head:

"God knows. He wasn't handsome, never worked as far as I know, had no ambition and no money except for a small inheritance he received just before they were married, which enabled him to build the house they still live in. The first two years of their marriage, you know, they went to dances at the courthouse and to the opera house for plays and musicals, then gradually Miss Minnie stopped going out at all, and it was rumored in town that all Bosie's inheritance money had been spent, his credit cut off by the merchants. Once in a while a neighbor would tell me that she had seen Miss Minnie walking up and down in her backyard for a half hour or so and then going back inside, and Bosie spent more and more time at the drugstore where he would take his seat early in the morning, and spend the rest of the day watching the customers, or talking over the weather, the crops or politics with one of his drugstore cronies. It was rumored in town that a relative of Miss Minnie's had died and left her some money, and everybody wondered if she would reappear, but she did not, becoming even more of a recluse, always now keeping the shades of her windows drawn. I tried to see her several times, walked once to her house and knocked, and I could hear the dogs yapping, but she wouldn't answer the door, so I gave up going."

"How old was she then?"

"Oh. I reckon forty. Yes. It was about nineteen ten and she would have been forty. Is it possible?"

"Nineteen ten?"

"Yes."

"I wasn't even born then."

"No, you weren't, bless your sweet heart."

"Then one day five or six years later, Bosie called to me as I was going past the drugstore, and said Minnie would like to see me. I was delighted of course and I told Bosie I would be over the next afternoon. Miss Minnie greeted me at the door, wearing a Mother Hubbard, her teeth all gone. She had aged a great deal, and surrounding her were five small yapping dogs. Now I'm scared to death of dogs, big or little, and Miss Minnie must have sensed that because she told the dogs to hush, and she said to me they won't bother you, Loula, just pay no attention to them, so I came on into the room and saw the house was in shambles and unkempt. It was all very upsetting. But she was gracious and talked as if we had visited only a few days before. She asked me a lot of questions, mostly about friends from her girlhood, and when the visit was over she said she hoped I would come again. She had no phone, said she would send a message by Bosie for a time for the next visit. I waited a year and there was no word from him, so I decided to call on her uninvited. I knocked on her door several times, and there was no answer, so I called out and said, Miss Minnie. It's Loula. Loula Horton. I knew she was inside, but there was no answer except the yapping of the dogs. A few years later a sister of Bosie's died and left him some money. He bought a car, and neighbors said once in a while in the late afternoon or early evening she would leave the house and ride with him around town."

"Do you ever try to see her now?"

"No, darling. She doesn't want to see me or anyone. She doesn't ever go riding anymore now, the neighbors say. Bosie leaves his car in the backyard shed. The neighbors say he can't afford the gas any longer."

I would go past Miss Minnie's house once in a while in the late twenties, thinking of my aunt's description of her, and wondering how she looked now, but I never got to see her.

Bosie died first, then Miss Minnie. I was away from Wharton then, and when I came home for a visit in the late thirties I asked my aunt about her.

"I guess your mother wrote you that she died," she said. "I almost wrote you, but I didn't. Time goes so fast, Sonny. I don't do half the things I mean to do. Well, I only know what the neighbors told me. She was alone when she died. The dogs' yapping turned to howls and the neighbors finally became alarmed and went into the house and found her dead."

"Was there a funeral?"

"Yes, and I went. There were only seven people there besides the preacher and no flowers except the ones I sent. My God, Sonny, my God. And she was a beauty. I can see her now in her green riding outfit, riding on her horse through town."

Part II

*These pictures of my father, Albert Horton Foote, Sr.,
and my mother, Harriet (Hallie) Gautier Brooks, were taken
in 1914, the year before their marriage.*

Chapter 6

My mother's father, Tom Brooks, was born in East Columbia in Brazoria County, Texas, in 1865 and came to Wharton in 1886. He was one of ten children born to John W. and Harriet Gautier Brooks. John Brooks had come to Texas from Virginia with his Smith uncles and cousins, and settled on the bank of the Brazos River.

Harriet Gautier's family had come from Florida, her family settling in the town of Brazoria, and they were close to Stephen Austin and his family. John Brooks died when my grandfather was five years old. A letter describing his death and sent to relatives back in Virginia reads:

Columbia, Texas, Oct. 7th, 1870

My Dear Aunt,

Surely the troubles of our family are great, too heavy to be borne, but for the help of a great and merciful God. Poor Uncle John how can I write that our dear, good uncle John, now rests under the sod. Too true it is, the evening of the 4th of this month, he breathed his last, and the next evening we followed his remains to the burying ground where he was interred. Tuesday, week, I went to uncle John's, found him sitting on the gallery, with his head resting on his hand. I asked him if he was sick, he said "Yes, I have had a chill, but thought that I felt well enough to go uptown, and started but had to come back." The next morning Nancy came down, a short time, and said that her papa was complaining, but was up. Sister A. went to see him in the evening, found that they had sent for a Dr. The Dr. found him very much congested, and he continued to get worse. Dr. Weems was absent at the time and did not get here until Saturday. We so much hoped that he would be able to do something when he came, but it appears that God had seen fit to have it otherwise. After feeling and hearing from the Drs. that there was little hope his wife nerved herself up and talked to him. She said "Mr. Brooks you are very sick," he told her "Yes" that he knew it, she then said "Mr. Brooks I hope that you will be spared, but in case that anything should happen, have you anything to say to me?" He said "Yes Harriet, there is a good deal that I would like to say, but I cannot talk well enough now. I must wait." She then said, "Mr. Brooks you must not forget in your sufferings to pray to God." He said "I do pray and often pray in my feeble way." The night before his death, the Drs. told his wife that if she wished to talk to him that she had better do so. She asked him if he was willing to die; he said no, that he could not say that he was willing to die. He had tried to do his duty, had prayed a part of every day, but could not say that he felt that material change that was spoken of. He had erred, he knew, but it was more an error of judgement than of the heart. His wife said "Mr. Brooks, you have been mighty good to me, we have been married near twenty years and have never had a quarrel, it was your goodness, not mine." He said no, I reckon not, there is not much good in me. She told him that he would have five of their children with him in heaven and she would have five with her. He said yes, if I am fortunate enough to get to the blessed place, and my number will gradually increase. She told him that she would try to bring their boys up to be just such men as he was. He said that he hoped that they would be better. Mr. S. talked with him and uncle John prayed aloud, a feeling prayer for himself and that God would bless us all, and at last bring us all to Heaven. His poor wife is stricken with grief, for a time she could not cry and I feared that she would go deranged. At times she looked so and would then calm herself and go back in the room and hang over uncle John, she would not leave him to sleep, but thank God, the last day tears came to her relief, and she now weeps in silence. The Masons buried uncle John and a large procession attended him to the grave. Uncle John gave Nannie some advice, told her that she must be a dutiful daughter to her mother, that he had always indulged her, but that he reckoned that they would have but little besides his life policy of $10,000 she must not fret because she could not live as she had done. Mrs. Brooks carried the baby to uncle John, and said Mr. Brooks our little baby has never been named. I want you to name it, what shall it be called, he said call her Laura, a name that the boys had given her from her birth. She was baptized by his corpse. You may imagine that a vacancy is caused in his family and indeed it seems to extend through the town. The men would say Dr.

"Brooks is too good a man to die, save him, he cannot be spared, he will be more missed than any other man in the place." He was loved by all.

In much love,
Laura Smith

Harriet Gautier, as a young girl, had gone to a fortune-teller and was told that she would be asked to marry a man who had come to Texas by boat, and that he would want to build a brick house for them, but she must refuse and insist on a frame house, else she would have an unhappy and tragic life. John had come to Texas by boat from Virginia, and when he proposed to Harriet he told her after they married he would build them a brick house, but remembering the warning of the fortune-teller, Harriet refused to marry him unless he built a frame house. He agreed and they were married in 1852.

Of their ten children, five died in infancy and those remaining were: Nannie, Peter Gautier, Tom, Billy and Laura. Tom, as a young man, was the most ambitious; received a scholarship to Texas A&M and graduated with honors.

Soon after graduation he moved to Wharton and clerked in an uncle's grocery store. Which he bought after a few years, taking Henry Cookenboo as a partner. In time my grandfather was elected county treasurer and served in that office from 1892 until 1906.

When he arrived in Wharton County in 1886 the old plantation system had been largely abandoned, for the freeing of the slaves and changing economic conditions made them financially impractical, and like a character out of *The Cherry Orchard* my grandfather began to buy up these abandoned plantations for little money, dividing them into small farms and selling them at great profit. He prospered in that and in all things and soon became a leader in the town and county.

He had been followed to Wharton by his older brother Peter Gautier, who became a banker, and by his younger brother Billy, who became a lawyer. He hired the first woman secretary in Wharton, my grandmother Mary Phelps Speed, called Daisy all her life.

Daisy was born in Brazoria County in 1868 on a plantation on Oyster Creek where her father, John Speed, was overseer. My grandmother went to work to support herself at an early age. Her first job was governess at one of the neighboring plantations and then she came to Wharton, where she was employed as a secretary.

She boarded at first in a house near the Hortons, the same house where my mother and father boarded many years later when they were first married, and she and the Horton girls became devoted friends.

She married my grandfather a year later and they had eight children. Two, Jenny Speed and Daisy, died in infancy. The six that survived were: Hallie (my mother), Laura Lee, Rosa Vaughn, Thomas Henry, John Speed and William Smith.

For whatever reason—it has been analyzed and reanalyzed many times in our family, and no conclusions reached—my grandfather didn't want any of his daughters to marry. His theories were simple and clear. Why should they marry when he could always provide for them? He could understand a man wanting to marry, but not a woman. He would point to all the unhappy marriages that were around them—women tied to worthless husbands with children to raise and care for, his sister, Nannie, forced by the early death of her husband to raise four children alone, in poverty. That he had an extremely happy marriage seemed never to alter his views. Also in obedience to the Methodist practice of the day none of the girls were allowed to play cards or dance.

Hallie had fallen in love early on with Syd Joplin, the manager of the local picture show, and had almost defied her father and eloped with him but, frightened by her father's opposition, she stopped seeing him, and he left town soon after.

She began seeing my father in the early spring of 1914. He was allowed to come to the house, until it became obvious that he and Hallie were seriously interested in each other, and then he was no longer welcome. Hallie pleaded with her father to change his mind, but he was adamant. He felt, he said, that my father was unworthy of her, that he was dissipated, impoverished, a ne'er-do-well. He told her, too, that it was all just infatuation and would pass in time. He cited Syd Joplin as an example of her fickleness.

Hallie continued to see my father, finding ways to meet him in the homes of her friends or at the picture show. Mrs. Cookenboo, the wife of my grandfather's partner, was the spy for the Brooks family and daily reported in great detail each of these clandestine meetings.

As I grew older I became more and more intrigued with the story of my mother, defying her parents, clandestinely meeting my father and finally eloping with him. My mother would talk about the plans for the elopement, the call to her father that the Baptist minister insisted she make, the way her father pleaded with her not to go through with the marriage, always repeating his same words: "Hallie, I beg you not to do this. You will regret it the rest of your life." In later years my father, however, refused ever to talk about it. He would listen as I questioned my mother for details, but would never add any of his own or answer any questions, except to say, "That's all in the past."

If my father was reluctant to talk about his elopement with my mother, or life with his father, there were topics he would hold forth on for hours. Every night after supper he and Mother would sit on the front porch of our house and go over the events of the day.

Their conversations began with Mother asking how business had been at the store. Why that question was ever necessary, I don't know, because my father, an extremely emotional man, usually signaled as he walked into our yard from town how that part of his day had turned out. If business had been poor he came home silent and depressed, and if it had been good, he was cheerful and outgoing.

But no matter how depressed he was when he arrived home, he most often, after seeing to his chickens or working in his garden and eating his supper, would go to the front porch and wait for my mother to join him after she finished her chores for the night. Here, he would begin with one of his favorite subjects, what he had learned from reading in the day's newspapers (he was an avid newspaper reader, often subscribing to as many as four).

"I swear, hon, I don't know what the world's coming to, I read in *The New York Times* today that some Bolshevik [his term for anyone he disapproved of] wants to break off all our alliances with England [he was always a fervent Anglophile]."

My mother would answer as if she had just heard the world was coming to an end, "You don't mean it."

"I do mean it. It makes me doggone mad, when some jackass goes on like that. I tell you right now I'd had anything to do with it, we'd never left the British Crown; the day we got our independence from England was to me a sad day. If we were still under a king or a queen we wouldn't be having to put up with all the dirty politics that we have now in our government."

Then he would go on to more local concerns.

"It was so dead in town today, nobody was doing any business. I went five times to the post office just so I could check on the other stores, and they were all empty, not one had customers."

"Well, don't get discouraged, hon."

"It's hard not to get discouraged, hon."

"I know, hon, but try not to."

"I try."

"I know you do."

Inevitably, though, he would find a way to take the conversation to his remembered past, to the days of "Old Wharton."

My mother, an artful listener and straight man, would softly punctuate his monologues with "I declare," or "Uh-huh," or "You don't mean it."

His tales of the past would often begin like this:

"Hon, do you remember when the Pridgens lived in the house the Dicksons live in?"

"Uh-huh."

"Where are they now?" he would ask, then answering his own question: "Living in Corpus. Aren't they?"

"Uh-huh."

"That's right. I remember hearing the other day that's where they were living. Were Gladys and Louella Pridgen older or younger than you?"

"Older."

"That's right. Who was older, Gladys or Louella?" Then again answering his own question, "Gladys, I believe."

"Uh-huh," again from my mother.

"They were both lovely dancers, you know. I went with Gladys for a while. Oh, way back, before I dated Ollie Elmore. One time when I was taking Gladys to a dance, a Christmas dance, I believe, at the courthouse. Everybody in town was going. An' there was a big Baptist revival the same night, and I said to Gladys, I think it would be a nice thing to do if we went to the revival meeting before we go to the dance, and she thought it was a lovely idea too, so we talked it over with the other couples, Archie and Allie, and Rita and whoever her date was, and I think Louella and her date, and they agreed, so we all went together to the revival meeting. The men all had on their tuxes and the ladies were in their evening dresses. We hardly had a chance to sit down good when Sissie Nelson and four or five other fanatical fools ran over to us and got down on their knees, and began crying and pleading with us not to go to the dance, saying that dances were sinful and the work of the devil. Did I ever tell you about that?"

"I think so."

"Shoot. We were all disgusted let me tell you."

"What did you do?"

"Got up and left them on their knees begging and pleading. Went to the dance and had a wonderful time."

(A pause, while he would light up his pipe.)

"You know what I was thinking about this afternoon in the

67

store? I don't know why. I was sitting by the front and all of a sudden I began to wonder where the Roseberrys are now."

"I wonder."

"How long since they've lived here?"

Again he answers his own question, "Fifteen years?"

"All of that."

"Yes, all of that. Maybe twenty. My God. Twenty years. Willie Roseberry was my best friend when I was growing up. I'd do anything for him, and he'd do anything for me. Who did you consider your best friend?"

Again he answers his own question, "Clark Davidson?"

"Yes."

"She was sixteen when she died, wasn't she? This whole town mourned."

Then he would begin to wonder at the sad fate of so many of their friends.

"My God," he would sigh dolefully. "It makes you humble when you think of what can happen to people. Archie Elmore blowing his brains out. Poor devil. Why would he do something like that?"

I would often be listening from my bedroom next to the porch and I would want to call out, "Wasn't his house the one you got married in?"

But before I could, he would go on to the next tragedy.

"And Rita, that no-good husband of hers, killing her father. He said it was in self-defense, that the poor old man was coming after him with a butcher knife. I don't believe that at all. Do you? A no-good rascal. I knew it when I first met him. Why in the name of God did Rita ever marry him? Some things I will never be able to understand."

I had been told that my grandparents had objected to my father because he was wild—that as a young man, he drank and gambled. In the anonymity of darkness and while I could hear he was in a contemplative, confessional mood, I would have liked to call out and ask if it was true. Had he ever been wild like his friends he often talked about? I never got the courage, though, and it was impossible really to believe that this hard-working, devoted family man had ever been anything but responsible.

My father never discussed his mother or sister or stepfather. His mother came to Wharton several times a year to see her sisters, and she would always come out for an afternoon to visit with my mother. I began to notice that my father managed to stay at his store until his mother had gone. I asked my mother about this, and she said he had a miserable childhood, that he had been abandoned by his mother when she married his step-father, leaving him to be raised by his grandparents, taking his sister to live with her in Houston.

"Why did she do it?" I asked.

"I guess it really wasn't her fault. I guess it was his stepfather, Mr. Cleveland, that made her leave him in Wharton. He's a very peculiar man, honey. He had gone to work as a boy supporting himself back in Atlanta, Georgia, after the war, and that's what he thought boys should do. Later, when your father somehow got enough money to go to business school in Houston for six weeks, he rented a room near his mother. She had made it clear that she couldn't ask him to stay with her, but she said she would be able to fix him a good breakfast every morning if he waited until his stepfather left for work. He said one morning he went over to have his breakfast and his mother came to the door and she seemed very nervous and she said, thank you, Son, for bringing the eggs, I do appreciate it. He said he had no eggs and didn't know what she was talking about, but when he looked into the house and saw his stepfather, he knew that his mother was afraid to tell him she was giving her son breakfast."

My mother would sigh and then say, "Oh, I don't know, Son, his mother is a good woman, but she just wasn't very sensitive. Your father told me that when she first separated from his father, she and his aunt Reenie opened a boardinghouse. He had been given some chickens, which he treasured, and took special care of. I guess his mother and his aunt were having a difficult time making ends meet. One day they were short of money and when he was away at school, without telling him, they killed all of his chickens for the boarders' supper. When he came home and found out he said he became desperately ill, and none of the doctors could figure out what was wrong."

"Do you think that's why he likes raising chickens so much today?"

"I guess so. I know the first thing he said when he moved here was that he wanted to raise chickens, if I didn't mind. Of course, I didn't. He had so little growing up. He told me as a boy all he ever got for Christmas was a piece of fruit. An orange or a banana."

"Did you get more than that at Christmas?"

"I sure did. Dolls and dollhouses, tricycles and bicycles, pretty dresses, oh, so much more."

After my father finished his business course, he got a job as a traveling salesman. He was only on the road, as he called it, for two years. His territory was East Texas, Arkansas, Louisiana and

Mississippi, and it was two years he never forgot. Often those nights on our porch he would begin one of his stories, "When I was on the road I used to . . ." Even at the end of his life, he made it sound like it had all happened yesterday.

Part III

Sycamore Grove—my great-great-grandfather Horton's plantation house.

Chapter 7

I have seen so many changes in this little town—not so little now, however, as when I was growing up. It was three thousand then, with almost as many blacks as whites. I knew all the whites, at least by sight, and I knew many of the blacks by their given names: Stant, Baby Clegg, Delia, Celleste, Little Bit, Willie, Dee and Walter. Walter was Stant's cousin, and looked almost white. I wondered about that, but never asked why it was so.

As a child I loved Stant. He was unmistakably black, but not black black like Dee, who worked for the Wilsons and at the cotton gin, to whom I also felt close.

Stant worked for my father when he had his first business, a cleaning and pressing shop, where he also took orders for tailor-made suits. He had samples of various suit materials in his shop and his customers would look through the samples and select the color and the kind of fabric they wanted their pants or suit to be, and he would take their measurements and send them off to the J. L. Taylor Company in Chicago, and in a few weeks their pants or suit would be sent back fully tailored and ready to be worn. I have no real memory of my father's shop, or even of my father at that time, but I have a distinct memory of Stant. I even knew his last name—Powell.

I remember always feeling very safe and secure with him, for no matter how busy he was he always paid me a great deal of attention. Sometimes carrying me around in his arms, calling me his boy, and bragging on me, making me feel very loved, and I thought he would surely be a part of my life forever. After a while, my father sold his cleaning and pressing shop and opened a men's store ("Men's Haberdashery," his letterhead said), and Stant went to work for someone else. After I got older and would meet him in town he would always greet me effusively, and I still felt this great affection for him. I left town at sixteen to go to Dallas to work and study acting, and when I returned home for a summer visit he had vanished.

I inquired about him once or twice, but no one knew where he'd gone, and so I stopped asking. He had always called me "Little Horton," and then one summer I saw him again and this time he called me "Mr. Horton" and that made me feel strange. I asked my father why he had done that and he said: "That's because you're both in the South and that's how things are done in the South." I didn't understand his answer then, but I accepted it and didn't ask any more questions. I never saw him again. I've often thought of him, and once in a while I would inquire about him, but could find no one that even knew him. He had vanished and so have many of the blacks I knew and felt close to as a boy.

Dee Wilson, one always called him Dee Wilson because he worked for Mr. Wilson, a white man who ran the cotton gin and the oil mill. Besides working at the gin and oil mill he took care of the Wilsons' yard and fields and milked their cows and did whatever chores they needed to have done.

The Wilsons owned five acres across from my grandparents' house, and as I got older, I spent almost every day in the summer playing there with Thurman, their middle son.

The Wilson acreage ran all the way across Caney Creek, by now drained, down to the cotton gin, and we spent our summers digging caves and building tree houses in the pecan trees. I was reading *Tom Sawyer* and *Huckleberry Finn* by then and I identified with them both, especially Tom, and his cave adventures. Dee was forever around it seems and patient he was too, always willing to help, or loan us a pick or shovel to dig caves, and find boards to help us shore up the caves after they were dug. He wanted to teach me how to milk a cow, but I wasn't interested, but I loved to hear him talk and tell his stories. His stories were almost as gifted and magical as those of Walter, not Stant's cousin, but another Walter, who was chauffeur and yardman for my grandmother and had been sent overseas in the First World War, and had seen mermaids (mare maids he called them) rise out of the ocean as he was crossing the Atlantic on his troop ship. Walter also had the gift of second sight. He could see spirits that no one else in his family (except his older sister Eliza, who cooked for my grandmother) could see and he was proud of his gift and would spend hours describing what he had seen. The most impressive of his stories to me was the time he and his sister, and the rest of his family, were going to church in their buggy, when suddenly the horse pulling the buggy began to rare and pitch and no one in the buggy except him and Eliza knew what was happening.

"What was happening?" I would always ask as if I didn't know the answer.

"Why there was a fiery chariot right there in the middle of the road facing us and they wouldn't go a step further until that chariot disappeared."

"Does Dee know about this?" I asked.

"Dee who?"

"Dee Wilson. That works for the Wilsons."

"He's a deacon," he answered.

"What does that mean?"

"He's sanctified."

I couldn't wait for milking time to ask Dee what sanctified meant, and what a deacon was. Dee seemed pleased at my interest.

"A deacon," he said, "is an officer in the church. That you're elected to."

"Is it like a preacher?"

"No, but I have preached and a good deacon is ready to preach when called on."

"And what does it mean to be sanctified?"

"It means you give up all worldly ways, no gambling, no drinking, no messing around with women after you're married, no swearing, go to church all day Sunday."

"You do all that?"

"I try to."

And I'm sure he did, for he was kindness itself. He was never too busy to listen to our troubles or help us solve whatever we couldn't figure out ourselves, whether it was building a tree house, making slingshots (nigger shooters we called them, without any embarrassment or awareness of the ugliness of the word) or peeling stalks of sugarcane for us to eat.

After I outgrew tree houses and digging caves and stopped going to the Wilsons', and I began to clerk in my father's store, he would come in every Saturday to buy clothes, or just to visit. My father always called him Deacon, and I began to call him that too. One Saturday he didn't come in and I called the Wilsons to inquire about him and I was told he was dead. I keep thinking they said he died in church, but I'm not really sure about that and the Wilsons are all gone now so I have no one to ask if it is true or not.

Walter and his sister Eliza each had a one-room house in my grandparents' backyard. I wonder now how they endured their lives so without complaint.

Eliza had to be up every morning (seven days a week) at seven and cook breakfast, dinner and supper. For all this she was paid three dollars a week, and furnished a one-room house and food. Walter worked in the yard, and after my grandfather died, chauffeured my grandmother on trips to the farms, the cemetery to visit my grandfather's grave, around town or to Houston. I never knew what he got paid, but I feel sure it was only three dollars too.

It was my uncle Billy's duty to wake Eliza if she overslept, and many a winter morning when she did, you could hear Billy calling from his back gallery, "Eliza. Eliza. Wake up. It's seven o'clock. Eliza. Eliza. Wake up, Eliza," and then in desperation if she hadn't responded, "Eliza, you ought to be ashamed of yourself. Wake up. Wake up. Mama, Papa. She won't wake up." Sometimes, from our back porch, my father would answer in a high falsetto, "Yes, Mr. Billy. I'm awake." And Billy would answer in a fury, "Shut up, Big Horton."

When my grandparents or my parents were too busy to talk to

me, I would often seek out Eliza and Walter. They did most of the talking, telling me about their family, the life they had as children on the farm they grew up on. Why they preferred living in town.

They took off every Sunday afternoon, after Eliza had cooked the Brookses' dinner, for the church in the country they had gone to all their lives.

Eliza's sister Sarah worked for a neighbor family. I was visiting with Eliza one night when Sarah came into her house visibly upset.

"Eliza?" she said. "Oh, Jesus."

"What's the matter, Sarah?" I asked.

"I can't tell you."

"Why can't you tell me?"

"Because you'll tell it and get me into bad trouble."

"I won't tell it."

"You swear?"

"I swear."

"All right, then. Sister?"

"What?" Eliza said.

"You know what just happened?"

"What?"

Sarah turned again to me.

"Swear you won't say anything?"

"I swear."

"Well, I was in the kitchen fixing supper when the missus came in from a trip to Houston, and she begin to holler at the mister, and I never heard such carrying on in my life. Some white woman who went into Houston with her told her her husband had been having an affair with a white lady."

"What was her name?" Eliza asked.

"I couldn't make out her name. She was crying and hollering all at the same time, and then they both got quiet and he said he loved this white lady and wanted a divorce, and she began hollering again that he ain't gettin' a divorce and then she called her children in and told the children, I want to tell you what kind of a man your father is—an' she told 'em everything."

"What did they say?" Eliza wanted to know.

"I couldn't hear. Someone got up and closed the door then. Swear, Little Horton, not to breathe a word of this, not to your mama, or your grandma."

"I swear."

The next day I heard my mother and grandmother discussing it, and I went to Eliza in the kitchen.

"Eliza?"

"Yes?"

"My mother and grandmother know all about what happened last night. Who told them?"

"Sarah."

"Sarah?"

"Yes, after you left she wanted a glass of water and we went into the kitchen to get a drink and your grandma was in the kitchen fixing a sandwich for Mr. Tom because he was hungry and Sarah swore her to secrecy too, and told her the whole thing."

Every so often after that Eliza would tell me what Sarah was telling her, about what went on in the house. The husband, a prominent businessman, lived on with his wife and children, but they wouldn't speak to him, or eat meals with him. He became ill, finally bedridden, and Sarah would take his meals to his bed, but neither his wife nor his daughter and son would go near him.

My talks with Eliza, Sarah and Walter were rarely about such dramas, but mostly about their church services, and news of their friends, none of them that I knew, but because of what they would tell me about them in such vivid detail, I felt I knew intimately.

Later, after Eliza and Walter had gone, they were replaced by Idella and her six-year-old daughter, Katie Belle, that Idella for some reason called Moot. Eliza was a wonderful cook, but Idella was even better, and I enjoyed my visits with her and Moot in their tiny house after the dishes were done and she had left the kitchen for the night. Idella didn't talk about church or her friends or her past life, but of the white people she had worked for, embellishing all of them with great wealth and power and influence. Later when I would ask my grandmother about some of the people, she would say she's making it all up. In truth, she said, most of them could hardly keep their heads above water.

On the Christmas day when I got my horse from my uncle Brother, Idella and Katie Belle joined us in the yard to admire it. My brothers each took turns riding on the horse while my father held the reins, leading them around the yard. We asked Katie Belle if she would like a ride and she said she would, Idella adding, you don't have to lead her around, she knows all about horses. But that was a fragment of Idella's fantasy; she didn't, and no sooner was she on the horse than it took off, full gallop, Idella screaming and Katie Belle screaming.

When I was a junior in high school, I was asked by a cousin, Robert Abell, to write a story for him. He was a freshman at the

University of Texas and was failing English, but was told if he turned in a short story of any worth, he still might be passed. He said he had come to me because I was always reading books and he figured for that reason I could write a story. I explained that I had never written one, but would try. I wrote one called "A Pinch of Salt," and it was about Eliza and Walter, although its details I've long since forgotten. When I finished it, I gave it to Robert and he turned it in to his professor. The next week he came home elated. Not only had the teacher liked the story and agreed to pass him, he had said, "Mr. Abell, I know you wrote it, because it is about niggers and you talk just like a nigger." It was another ten years, however, before I was to ever try writing again.

There was one black that I was in terror of when I was a small child. He was called "Loping Jody" or the "Horse Nigger" because he always loped instead of walking and he couldn't talk, but would make strange guttural noises as he went. He stayed mostly in the black section across the tracks. The ice house was located there and when my uncles would drive over to pick up extra ice, they often offered to take me along. I loved to ride in cars and I would always accept, though I knew all too well what might happen when we got over there if Loping Jody was in sight, because the minute they saw him my uncles would grab me and hold me up and call to him to come and get me. Poor simple thing, wanting to please, would come loping over, holding out his arms and making his guttural sounds, and I would scream in terror, much to the delight of my uncles. As I got older I realized he was harmless, and as he passed our store, my father would speak to him. I asked my father how he lived and who took care of him, but my father didn't know. He just got along somehow, he said.

Also afflicted were Charlie Rugeley and Arthur St. John, both white.

Arthur lived with his parents outside of Wharton in the country. They had no car, which he couldn't have driven if they had, and he would stand for hours on the road outside his house waiting for someone he knew to come along and take him into town. Once in town he would walk up and down the streets, stopping to talk whenever someone called to him. He was teased by boys and older men unmercifully at times, but he seldom got angry and would laugh when they did at his foolish answers to their questions.

One of the favorite sports of these older men would be to tell him that certain popular girls in town had a crush on him and give him a nickel to call them and ask for a date.

Charlie Rugeley, a nephew of Great-Aunt Peg Brooks, was as nervous and jittery as Arthur was serene and calm. He rode a bicycle and delivered telegrams for Western Union. He kept his bicycle when not in use chained to a post in front of Outlar's Drugstore and one of the favorite sports of the men hanging around the drugstore was to find a way to make the bicycle difficult to get loose from the post. Charlie had a terrible temper and at the least resistance to freeing his bicycle, he would fly into a rage, kicking the bicycle and muttering curses. After watching his fits (as they called them) for a moment or so, one of the men, suppressing his laughter, would help him get his bicycle free.

Once my mother and daddy and I were going into Outlar's Drugstore for a Coke and we saw Charlie riding up on his bicycle. Mother spoke to Charlie as we passed him and he didn't answer.

"Mother?"

"Yes, Son?"

"Everybody says Charlie is Aunt Peg Brooks's cousin. Is he our cousin too?"

"No, Son. We're kin to Aunt Peg by marriage, but that doesn't make her blood relatives our kin."

"Well, never mind about Charlie," my father said. "He makes a living for himself, which is more than I can say for those hooligans that have nothin' better to do than to think of ways to get him into a fit. And I'll tell you a sad thing. Charlie was normal as a young man, but then he had a spell of fever and it left him nervous and simpleminded."

"Is that what happened to Arthur St. John too?" I wanted to know. "Did he have a fever of some kind too?"

"No, he was born simpleminded."

I once got up the courage to speak to Charlie. He wouldn't look at me when I called his name, or answer when I asked how he was feeling. Instead he muttered insensibly to himself. One didn't have to approach Arthur, he approached anyone he met on the street, usually telling them about the latest girl who had a crush on him.

Chapter 8

We had no neighbors on our street until I was four, when my grandfather sold a lot directly across from us to the Charlie Joplins, who had two children at the time, Edwin and Mary Beth. Edwin was my age and we soon became close friends.

Mr. Charlie, as I called him, was a contractor, and he designed and built his own house. It was of stucco, a rarity in our town of mostly frame houses. He was from East Texas, though his wife, Miss Ida, was born in Wharton and lived as a girl for a while in a house on Richmond Road next to my grandparents' house, a house later owned by Miss Maggie Watts, and like so many houses on Richmond Road now torn down. A filling station is in its place.

Later, two of Mr. Charlie's nephews came from East Texas to work for him. They stayed in a small room over the Joplins' garage. How they could stand living there in the heat of the summer was a constant wonder to my parents.

My grandparents had many neighbors on their street, Richmond Road, which ran from the river bridge through town to the Santa Fe tracks, then became the highway to Houston.

Whenever I visited my grandmother I would question her about who owned what house.

"Baboo?"

"Yes, honey."

"Who owns the house across the street?"

"Which one?"

"The one that's white and two-story and has two galleries and the columns."

"The Outlars live there now, but we still call it the Dockery house."

"Why do you call it that?"

"Because the Dockerys lived there when we first bought this house. When we came in the neighborhood the Outlars lived in that cottage next door where the Wilsons live now."

"Mr. Wilson owns the cotton gin and the oil mill."

"I don't think he owns them, darling. I just think he manages them, and you know the Dockerys didn't build their house but bought it when Mr. Henry Bolton got in all that trouble and had to sell it."

"What trouble did he get into?"

"I'll tell you about it someday when you're older. And Mr. Aldredge and Mae lived in the house next to ours where the Giffords used to live."

"What happened to the Aldredges?"

"Well, that's a long story, darling. I'll tell you that, too, when you're older."

"The Cookenboos live next to the Wilsons," I said, pointing to their house.

"That's right," my grandmother said.

"John B. is their son?"

"One of their sons. They have two more. Ellwood and Henry."

"Where are they?"

"They work in Houston now."

"I heard Mrs. Cookenboo say Mr. Cookenboo likes to eat."

"That's true. No sooner has he finished breakfast than he says to Mrs. Cookenboo, what's for dinner, switheart?"

"Why does he say switheart?"

"Because that's how he pronounces sweetheart, and as soon as he finishes dinner then he says, what's for supper, switheart."

"I heard Papa say he'd hate to have to pay their grocery bills."

"I know."

"Is Mrs. Cookenboo your best friend?"

"Yes, in many ways."

My aunt Rosa once told me that when my grandmother knew she was pregnant with Billy, her eighth child, she and Mrs. Cookenboo would go into her bedroom and close the door, and my aunt said she could hear my grandmother crying in despair over the thought of another child and Mrs. Cookenboo comforting her.

When Mr. Cookenboo died he left very little savings. Mrs. Cookenboo sold their house, and left for Houston with John B. My grandmother often helped them financially and loaned John B. the money to go to business school. He became a very successful Houston businessman and my grandmother always spoke of his accomplishments with great pride. My mother used to marvel at her capacity to take pride in the success of her friends' sons, never complaining at the injustice of her own sons turning out so badly.

I kept thinking about Mr. Henry Bolton and his troubles and

two days later I asked my mother what he had done that got him into trouble.

"How do you know about Mr. Henry Bolton?"

"Baboo told me, but she wouldn't say how he got into trouble."

"Oh."

"She wouldn't tell me about Mr. Aldredge either."

"Well, I'll tell you someday."

"When?"

"When you're older."

"Please tell me now, Mother."

"Well, all right, but you have to promise not to tell any of your friends."

"I promise."

"Well, at one time the president of the Security Bank was Mr. Henry Bolton and the vice president was his son-in-law. Mr. Aldredge was married to Miss Mae Bolton."

"Was I born then?"

"No, all this happened before I was married to your daddy. I was still living with Mama and Papa. The first time our family suspected all was not well with the Aldredges is when we saw them going out every night in their buggy, carrying a lantern, and not returning home until early next morning. It turned out that Mr. Aldredge had made many unwise loans to farmers in the county and because of crop failures they could not meet their payments, so he was desperately going out at night, from farm to farm, trying to collect some of the owed money. He was unable to, and the bank failed. When the books of the bank were examined improprieties were uncovered and both Mr. Aldredge and his father-in-law, Mr. Henry Bolton, were accused of misappropriating funds. Mr. Bolton and Mr. Aldredge both protested no wrongdoing and accused the other as responsible for any misdeeds. There was a trial, a bitter one, and Miss Mae and her mother sided with Mr. Aldredge against their father and husband. Both men, however, were found guilty of fraud and sent to the penitentiary. Miss Mae and her mother were left penniless and Mrs. Bolton sold her house to the Dockerys and Miss Mae hers to George Gifford, the president of the rival bank. The women left town. Mrs. Henry Bolton never returned. Miss Mae came back briefly, a few years later, asking former friends to sign a petition for paroling her husband. No one would. Mr. Henry Bolton came back once, too, after he had gotten out of the penitentiary. He came in on the early train from Houston, visited with a few loyal friends and then took the afternoon train out of town and was never seen again. It was a sad time, honey. A sad time. You see that vacant lot there? That's where Mr. Aldredge's house used to be."

"What happened to it?"

"Oh, it's another sad tale. Like I told you Mr. Gifford bought the house from Miss Mae and he lived there with his family for a number of years. He had also extended credit to farmers and among them was a Mr. Hood, who had a large plantation, was his best friend and was heavily in debt to the bank. Mr. Gifford felt finally he had to foreclose and take his friend's plantation. This enraged Mr. Hood and as Mr. Gifford was coming out of the bank he shot and killed him. It was your grandmother who had to go to Mrs. Gifford and tell her what had happened. She said it was one of the most difficult things she ever had to do, and that when Mrs. Gifford saw her as she came into the room, she said, what is it? Is there something wrong with Mr. Gifford?"

Chapter 9

I was always very close to my grandmother and grandfather Brooks. Papa, as I called my grandfather, echoing his children, was plump, slightly bald, with an infectious laugh. I've been told by my mother and aunts that he also was an incurable tease, but I was never subjected to that side of him.

My grandmother I called Baboo. I gave her that name myself, as a child, and presume that my name for her grew out of my trying to say grandmother; in any case that is all I ever called her, and the name was later adopted by the other grandchildren.

My grandmother, like my mother, had never been called by her Christian name, but was always called Daisy.

She was a small, petite woman, always fashionably dressed and with a great flair for decorating the houses and apartments she lived in during her eighty-six years. Yards, too, were transformed by her with the help of willing and, under her spell, often enthusiastic yardmen.

She was indulged and pampered in all ways by my grandfather and when he died there was fear in the town and among her children that she would be unable to manage the farms and money left to her. She did manage, though, in fine style, and at her death the estate she had been left by her husband had increased considerably.

Since our houses were so close, I spent as much time with my grandparents as with my mother and father. I always felt loved and welcomed by them, and one of the most pleasant and persistent memories of my boyhood was riding with them in their green Studebaker to check out their cotton farms scattered over the county.

The roads to the farms were dirt, gravel or shell (mostly dirt), and it was difficult to visit the farms all in one afternoon, or even one day, since every farm visited meant getting out of the car and talking with the tenants, inquiring about their health, the health of their wives and children, and walking out into the fields to inspect the present state of the cotton or corn crop.

One farm we visited often didn't belong to my grandfather, but to Sarah Edwards, a black lady of ample proportions, with a loud, raucous voice, who always talked in a shout as if we were all deaf. We never left her farm without gifts: eggs, a chicken, a turkey, whatever fresh vegetables were in season—butter beans, turnips, okra, corn, mustard greens, peas, turnip greens, Irish or sweet potatoes.

My grandfather would inspect her crops as carefully as he did his own, and she would declare more than once during our visits that it was with the help of God and Mr. Tom Brooks that her farm had not been taken from her. Evidently, she had gotten in debt to the bank and when they were about to foreclose, asked my grandfather for help. He took over her note from the bank and gave her manageable time to pay it off. Once, her front yard was all plowed up and when I asked her why, she said someone had tried to conjure her, and she had to dig up her yard to find the conjure.

The tenants on my grandfather's favorite farm were the Kendalls. It was a thousand acres, with only a part in cultivation, live oaks and native pecan trees in abundance on the rest.

The Kendalls, my grandfather would always declare, were born farmers and their land and crops were always free of Johnson grass that, all too often, choked out cotton and corn on the farms of lazy or indifferent farmers.

Kendall, a lean black man, had little to say on our visits, though he was pleasant enough in answering a direct question from my grandfather. His wife, Maud, made up for his reticence. A small, wiry woman, with a great deal of energy and two gold front teeth, she was or had been a schoolteacher, I can't remember now which, but she was proud of that fact and usually found a way to tell you that.

To get to these farms, seven in all, we would pass tiny, dwindling towns named Iago, Burr, Glen Flora, Lane City, Egypt, Hungerford. Every now and then we would ride twenty-five miles to East Columbia in Brazoria County, where my grandfather was born. When I was growing up, there was a photograph in my house, and in the houses of my aunts and grandparents, of a large, impressive house that stood on the banks of the Brazos River, with a circle of live oaks in the front yard. Also in the yard were a number of children and three adults, some of them playing a game of croquet. This was the home of my grandfather's parents, a house he lived in until he went off to college. It was abandoned and finally taken down after his mother died and the other children moved away to other towns. The photograph hangs in my house today.

All that remained now of East Columbia were seven houses; an abandoned store, where my grandfather had worked as a boy and a young man, and a cluster of diminishing live oaks where once my grandfather's house stood. I would try to reconstruct that house, imagining the day my aunts, uncles and cousins were photographed in front of it, standing primly dressed in their best clothes. Some of them were dead now and those who were living returned to East Columbia with their children and grandchildren as infrequently as we did, gathering mostly for weddings and funerals.

And so, riding around with my grandparents, and passing these dwindling and forgotten towns, "why" was added to my vocabulary. Why did this town never prosper? Why was it never more than a church, a grocery store and one or two houses? Why did the people leave this town and go to another place? Why?

My grandfather would patiently explain how towns came to be and for what purpose; how circumstances changed so that towns were abandoned. He said that the railroad in the beginning almost went through Glen Flora instead of Wharton, and if that had happened, why . . . Then he would pause and we would all contemplate what that would have meant. For Wharton in those days, God knows, was no metropolis, but it was the county seat; we had the courthouse, a respectable Main Street, two railroad stations and three cotton gins. If Glen Flora had gotten the railroad instead of Wharton, it would have the Main Street, the courthouse, the two depots.

One of the pleasures of making films of mine that were set in Texas was riding around with the director and art director, looking for towns that might help establish a sense of late-nineteenth-century and early-twentieth-century Texas, towns like Waxahachie, Palmer and Ennis.

One of my favorites is Venus, in northeast Texas. We used it for two of my films, *1918* and *On Valentine's Day.* Its Main Street has a number of brick buildings, half of them in use, the rest abandoned. On one corner is a brick building that had been the local bank, and was used as one of the banks held up in the film *Bonnie and Clyde.* Venus had once been a prosperous cotton town, but cotton has moved on, and so have the people.

Thinking of those abandoned houses and towns, I am reminded of these lines from Robert Frost's poem "Directive":

> *There is a house that is no more a house*
> *Upon a farm that is no more a farm*
> *And in a town that is no more a town.*

Chapter 10

My maternal grandmother, because of the death of her two older siblings in the 1890s, was now the oldest of the living Speed children and her brothers and sisters looked to her in times of trouble.

I used to ask her about her childhood, but she would never talk about it much.

"Where was your plantation?" I asked her one day.

"It wasn't our plantation. We didn't have a plantation. My father was the overseer on a plantation."

"Where was that?"

"On Oyster Creek. My mother was a saint."

"What was her name?"

"Virginia Yerby Speed."

"What was your father's name?"

"John Speed."

"Was he a saint too?"

"No," my grandmother laughed. "I'm afraid not. To tell you the truth he was a moody, difficult man. When it rained, when the last thing the cotton needed to make any kind of crop was rain, my papa would not get out of bed, but would pull the covers over his head and stay there all day."

When her father could no longer work, and he had no savings, it was my grandmother and grandfather who took her parents into their home. They brought with them a lady's rocking chair (hers) and a platform rocker (his), and little else. My great-grandmother died first, and my great-grandfather continued to live with my grandparents for several years more until his death.

My grandmother had saved a pair of slippers that she had worn as a girl to a dance. There were two tiny bloodstains and holes on the soles of the slippers that were caused, she said, because she had danced all night, until dawn, without stopping.

She had been raised a Presbyterian, and had been allowed to dance. When she came to Wharton there was no Presbyterian church at the time, so she became a Methodist, the church my grandfather, though not a member, had been raised in. She became a devoted Methodist, active in the Missionary Society, attending church at least once on Sunday, and went to all the revival meetings. When the presiding elders came to town she entertained them at dinner.

She was loyal beyond belief to her brothers and sisters and to my grandfather's family, and it was to her they all came in times of trouble or tragedy. This same loyalty extended to cousins and in-laws and to her children and grandchildren. Indeed, while she was alive I had the secure feeling that if I ever needed anything I could call or write her to tell her of my need, and she would see to it that it was taken care of.

Part IV

My father's mother, Corrella Horton Cleveland. My father never cared for her second husband, Pete Cleveland, whom she married after his father's death.

Chapter 11

I was enrolled in the Wharton public school when I was five, and I've often wondered if I was sent at such an early age to make life easier at home for my mother, who was then pregnant with my brother Tom Brooks, born in November 1921. My brother John Speed was born two years later. Both of them, as I was, were born at home, but I have no memory of those events. How could I not be aware, with all the preparations that must have taken place? The baby beds, the baby clothes, the arrival of the doctor and midwife. Tom Brooks was born at two in the afternoon while I was at school; John Speed at five, when I should have been home, but probably was sent to my grandparents'. I have no memory, either, of being called to my mother's bedside and being shown a new brother.

I think now that I deliberately shut my brothers out of my consciousness. For five years I had been not only the center of my parents' attention and affection, but the only grandchild, and the first nephew, great-nephew and great-great-nephew in our extended family. I felt so the love and devotion of all these good, kind people that I'm sure I didn't want to ever share their attention and affection.

I've outlived them both. My brother Tom Brooks followed me

to New York in 1943 and was studying acting with my teachers Vera Soloviova and Andrius Jilinsky when he was drafted into the army. He became a radio pilot in the air force, and in 1944, his plane was shot down over Germany. He was reported missing in action. I was in rehearsal with my first Broadway play, *Only the Heart,* when I learned of this in a letter from my father.

Dear Son:

This morning I am sorry to say the first link in our little chain of five has been strained badly, but I will not yet say broken, for I have too much faith in God to give up that easy. We received a wire at 8:30 a.m. from the war department that Toots, was missing in action since Feb. 23rd in a raid over Germany. I still hope he is a prisoner. If not! and he has passed on of course the link in our little family chain of five has been broken, and we can only face the future with chins up, as we of course know he will meet whatever is beyond this life with clean hands, for I don't believe he ever did anything that hurt anyone here.

It has been much harder on mother here this morning than myself. You know how friends in a small town are, and we have lots of them. They have been pouring in home all morning to see her and offer sympathy. Son you would be proud of her if you were here and could see what a real sport she has shown through it all . . .

I know you are very busy at this time but am going to ask you to take a little time off and write mother at once, for she seems to get something out of your letters that nothing else can take the place of at this hour her heart is very heavy I assure you.

*   *   *

As a baby, Tom Brooks was curly haired and beautiful. There is a picture of the two of us dressed in costumes for a Valentine's Day tea given by the Methodist church. He is dressed as Cupid and I as Simple Simon, and in the picture I am striking a pose, trying to look the part. Many years later, feeling insecure and neglected for some reason, I asked my mother resentfully why she allowed me to go as Simple Simon. She said it was my choice. I heard so often, as we were growing up, that Tom Brooks was the beautiful one, then as we got older, the handsome one. By inference, it seemed to me that John Speed and I not only were not handsome, but lacked any distinction. So, I wonder now if I chose to be Simple Simon to send a signal that I knew I was inferior in my looks, but didn't care.

Because of the differences in our ages, I had little in common with my brothers, and tried to ignore them as much as possible, but one afternoon after seeing *Beau Geste* with Gary Cooper, a story about the devotion of three brothers to each other, I left the theater and ran home through the cotton fields as fast as I could, filled with a newfound love for my own brothers and swearing to myself that I would always be as devoted to them as Gary Cooper was to his brothers in the film. I found my brothers playing with Tinkertoys and I grabbed and hugged both. They looked at me like I was crazy and went back to their Tinkertoys.

Like all Southern schools at the time, the Wharton public school was segregated. We did have one Mexican boy, Estaquio Trevino, in my third-grade class, the only Mexican in school at the time, except for Peter May, who was adopted and raised by a white family living in a house near the graveyard. How the Mays came to adopt Peter I don't know, but they treated him with great kindness and as one of the family. The Mays had five children of their own, and Mr. May, as far as I know, never worked except for a few years when he sold pecans. My grandmother had a pecan cracker that Mr. May had invented, she said, but before he could get it patented, someone stole the idea from him and beat him to the patent. She said he never recovered from that disappointment. How the Mays lived with no one working I have no idea. It was the same for a number of families I knew where no one ever seemed to work, but they managed someway to live with some measures of comfort.

The New Wharton Independent School Building, as it was called, had been built a few years before I enrolled in the first grade, and stood at the north edge of town across the Santa Fe railroad tracks, where cotton fields began.

The schoolhouse was an uninviting two-story brick structure with enough classrooms to accommodate grades one to eleven. Set comfortably back from the shelled road, there was to one side a large yard leading on to a field where football and other athletic events were practiced and played. A bell rang announcing the beginning of classes, and rang again when it was time to leave. As I got older and was less diligent about being on time, I would sometimes be just crossing the Sante Fe tracks when the morning bell would ring and I would have to run full speed to the school yard in order not to be marked late.

Starting school at five meant I was going a year earlier than my neighborhood playmates, Thurman Wilson and Edwin Joplin, and I was the youngest in my class, two years younger than most.

School began in early September when the summer heat was still lingering and the temperature often hit ninety. Not that I noticed it. I played in the heat every summer, my mother only insisting that I rest, in the house, between one and three, while she took a nap. Sometimes I did, but more often after half an hour I was begging to go back outside, and she would agree as long as I promised to play under the trees, in our yard or my grandmother's, and stay out of the sun. I was obsessed in those days with tops and marbles and could amuse myself for hours with them, either in the house or out in the yard. I was also, at early age, given a pocketknife and became an expert at mumblety-peg. My favorite climbing tree was a giant pecan in the lot where my grandfather kept his horse. I had to nail boards to the trunk to help me get to the lower limbs. Once there I would climb almost to the top.

My first-grade teacher, Miss Oatman, was new in town and this was her first job. The first grade had been taught exclusively for a number of years by Mrs. Estill, but this year, because of increased enrollment, there were two sections.

There was a great deal of discussion about which first grade I was to be in. Most parents wanted their children with Mrs. Estill, a great town favorite, but for some reason my mother, usually shy and retiring, insisted on my being with Miss Oatman. Miss Oatman married two years later, and had to resign from teaching, as married women, except for Mrs. Estill, were not allowed in those days to continue in the Wharton school system. Why an exception was made for Mrs. Estill I never knew. Miss Oatman was a large-boned, hearty soul and stayed on in town after marrying, and even after, whenever she saw me, she would call out: "There's my boy."

I've tried to remember the names of my teachers in second and third grades, but I can't. I called the one person I knew who was in school at about the same time, and she, too, could only remember the names of the first-grade teachers. The present administration office at the school was of no help as they only had records from 1945. I remember one of the teachers, considered quite a beauty, except for her legs, which were stocky. When this defect was pointed out to me, it was the first time I realized legs could be different and judged as assets or liabilities. The lady became involved with one of the local bachelor merchants, and went for a ride on the river in his motorboat. Somehow the boat turned over and her legs were cut by the boat's motor. She sued him not only for damage to her legs, but for breach of promise, claiming he had vowed to marry her. I don't know how the suit was settled, but I do know she left town at the end of the school year, unmarried, and the whole affair caused a great deal of discussion between my parents and grandparents.

Teachers were paid very little and often shared a rented room in town with another teacher. No teachers could get time off except in case of sickness or very urgent business. Any teacher, man or woman, who got married was only permitted to finish the term. The school board also adopted a rule requiring teachers to consult the superintendent if they wished to go anywhere on a school night. The teachers were usually young, and just out of college.

Sometimes they married well and prospered, but often they didn't and in later years, when married women were allowed to teach school, many returned to teaching. Some, of course, never married, and stayed on teaching until they became too old to continue. There were no pensions in those days and salaries were low, but they continued to eke out a living someway, usually tutoring children that were having difficulties in school. The teachers were watched like hawks for any moral lapses. If they smoked it had to be in secret, and they were expected to attend church regularly. I remember an elderly lady who had been teaching many years. She became very involved with her students and often corresponded with them after they left Wharton. In a letter to a former student she made fun of one of the girls in her present class, implying that she was boy crazy. Somehow, the letter got into the hands of the girl's mother. There was a terrible scandal then and the poor teacher was hounded out of her job and had to leave town. I remember, too, one teacher telling us that the North was right during the Civil War. One of the students reported it to her parents and soon it was all over town. The teacher was called before the school board and instructed to tell her class that the South was right or else she would be fired.

Early on in school, I struck up a close friendship with two boys, Allison Dunn and Leslie Crockett, and we would play together on the school grounds and visit with each other after school. I knew Allison first. His mother and father were both dead and he had come to Wharton from Louisiana to live with his sister and her husband. I was never told the circumstances of his parents' death, but I often fantasized about it, imagining a car accident, typhoid fever, TB, and wondering what would become of me if my parents died.

Allison's brother-in-law had come to Wharton with an oil crew, and he and his wife lived in a rented house a half block from the graveyard. Allison's sister was about the age of my own mother, and was a sweet, gentle, soft-spoken lady who always made me feel welcome in their home.

I was at home reading one evening when Allison's sister phoned to say they were waiting supper on me. Had I forgotten I was invited to supper and that I had accepted? Yes, I had. She said the supper was for Allison's birthday. I had forgotten that, too, if I had ever been told. I had to put on a clean shirt and pants, in a hurry, and without a birthday present run as fast as I could the four blocks to their house. The supper: fried chicken, fried corn, English peas, rice and gravy, biscuits and birthday cake were on the table when I got there. I was the only guest, and though Allison's sister made nothing of the fact that I had forgotten the invitation, I was embarrassed and stricken with guilt. Allison's brother-in-law was transferred within the year to another county with oil prospects, and he and his sister followed soon after. I never heard from him again.

When I first knew Leslie Crockett, he lived with his family near the river in the oldest part of Wharton. They had moved here from the Texas Valley and his father was involved with raising and selling spinach and other vegetables that were beginning to be grown in the county. Leslie had a brother several years younger and a much younger sister. I don't remember ever seeing the father, but his mother was always around when I visited him at their river house, and was affable and a big talker. One day Leslie called and asked if I would like to spend a Saturday at his new house in the country. I accepted, and early Saturday he and his mother came for me in their car. She was her usual gracious self and we drove a mile or so out in the country to their new home. I stayed most of the day, and when I got back around six, my mother was waiting in the living room.

"Did you have a good time, Son?" she said.

"It was all right," I said.

"Son?"

"Yes, ma'm."

"A very sad thing has happened and if I tell you about it, you must never discuss it with anyone, especially with Leslie."

"Yes, ma'm. I won't."

"His father has left his mother for another woman. That's why she's moved out to the country. I hear he's asked her for a divorce, but she says she won't give him one until the children are grown."

I felt so sad for my friend, and puzzled, too, because he and his brother, his sister and his mother all seemed happy and cheerful that day. Soon after, they moved away from Wharton, and I never heard from Leslie again.

I wonder, now, why the memory of those two boys, of all I knew growing up, has stayed so with me. I think perhaps because it was the first time I'd heard of someone my age losing both parents and having to live with a sister and brother-in-law, or someone my age whose parents were divorced. After all these years, when I think of them, both towheads, and very thin, Allison quiet and calm, Leslie nervous, high-strung and a chatterer like his mother, I sense a great sadness about them. Perhaps though, I'm only imagining this, because in truth neither of them ever burdened me with their feelings or ever alluded to any unhappiness in their lives.

For my seventh birthday, my mother gave me a party after school and asked for a list of the boys and girls I wanted invited. I included my Mexican friend Estaquio Trevino.

I'm sure, in those far-off segregated days, that my mother wondered at the reaction of the other children and their mothers, but she said nothing of that to me. She did caution me not to be upset if he didn't come to the party, but he did. He was, I remember, the neatest-dressed boy there. He wore a white shirt, knickers, and had on a brand-new pair of tennis shoes that he told me his parents had bought just for the party. He disappeared from Wharton soon after and I never saw or heard from him again. I missed him though, because after Allison and Leslie left, we played together often during recess at school. If he had stayed on in Wharton he would have been taken out of the white school the next year and sent to the newly formed all-Mexican school whose classes were held in the old schoolhouse that my mother had gone to as a girl.

Chapter 12

I heard little classical music until I left Wharton. The most complicated piece I remember my mother playing on the piano was Ethelbert Nevin—"Narcissus." There was always around us music of a kind, though, certainly hymns and blues and what was called then race music. We could hear this music as we sat on our porch in the evenings. The blues and the race music would come to us from the flats, the name given a black section that was home to several barbecue restaurants and a barbershop for blacks on Caney Street. It would be joined, sometimes, far in the distance, by the sounds of a small Mexican band playing a Mexican waltz, or a neighborhood child practicing piano. The Baptist church was just a block away and these other musical sounds would be joined by their hymns on Wednesday evenings at prayer meeting time.

My mother was pianist and later organist for the Methodist church, and at an early age I attended church with her, both morning and evening services. Here I learned to sing and love many of the hymns: "Blessed Assurance," "Jesus Loves Me," "In the Sweet By and By," "Shall We Gather at the River?"

For a while my mother taught piano, and tried to teach me,

too, but gave up after two or three lessons when I refused to practice.

I learned the lyrics of many of the race songs by hearing them played over and over at night on the jukeboxes down in the flats. The lyrics of "Red Cap Porter," sung, I believe, by the Yas Yas Girl, or maybe Lil Green, both great favorites in the South at the time, are still with me.

> *Red cap porter*
> *Help me with my load*
> *Train's coming soon*
> *and I gotta get on board*

I remember my father had collected sheet music for popular songs since he was a young man and he brought them all with him when he married my mother. Often in the evenings, she would play, and he would sing, "Good Night, Mr. Elephant," "My Sweetheart's the Man in the Moon," "After the Ball" and "Hello, Central, Give Me Heaven." Before and after singing the latter he would tell how he had heard Chauncey Olcott, a famous singer when he was a young man, sing that song at the Wharton Opera House, always adding, "When he finished, there wasn't a dry eye in the house." Sometimes those sounds would come together all at once: the hymns from the Baptist church, the blues or race music from the flats, the Mexican waltzes, and later my brother John Speed would have the radio turned to a country-western station and that music would be added to the mix. I think that's why the music of Charles Ives has always meant so much to me. The sources he uses to quote in his symphonies and sonatas is often the kind of music I heard all around as I was growing up.

As I grew older, we like everyone else in our neighborhood had radios. I was allowed to listen only at certain hours. I chose to listen to Little Jack Little, with his theme song of "Little by Little," or Kate Smith, Bing Crosby, Rudy Vallee or Morton Downey. I knew, along with most of my classmates, all the popular songs of that day and time, and often sang or hummed them to myself.

My grandmother Brooks had a Victrola, and my uncle Brother, lovesick at the time, my family said, bought many records. I would often slip over to my grandmother's in the late afternoon and listen to Ruth Etting singing, "Ten Cents a Dance," Ethel Waters singing, "Am I Blue?" or Bing Crosby, part of a trio then, singing, "Mississippi Mud."

Some summers I visited Big Mama, my name for my paternal grandmother Cleveland, for a week in Houston. She had no radio, but she talked often of music and performers she had heard in Houston concerts: John McCormack, Gala Curchi, Paderewski, Alma Gluck, all strange names to me. She had an obvious love for these artists and their music, and though I never got to hear them, I remember her vivid descriptions of how they performed, the music they sang or played, and what it all meant to her.

Sometimes Big Mama took me to visit her daughter, my aunt Lily, and it wouldn't be long before she asked: "Did Mama tell you I had composed another piece last week?"

"No, I didn't," Big Mama nervously answered. (She was obviously afraid of Aunt Lily.) "I was too busy asking about Wharton. Why don't you play your piece for him?"

"Do you like music, sweetheart?" my aunt inquired. "I mean classical music. Chopin, Mozart, Liszt?"

"I don't know if I do or not. I don't think I've ever heard any of it," I answered as politely as I knew how.

"Doesn't your mother play for you?"

"Yes, she plays sometimes after supper, and my daddy sings."

"What kind of music?"

" 'My Sweetheart's the Man in the Moon' and—"

"Trash. That's trash, darling," my aunt smirked.

"Now, Sister," Big Mama said diplomatically, "you used to compose rags, and I don't know to this day why some music publisher hasn't bought that song of yours, 'I'm Just a Square Peg in a Round Hole.' That song of yours would make a fortune."

"I'm not interested in that kind of trashy music anymore, Mama."

"I know you're not, Sister, I only meant it could make somebody rich. Why don't you play your new étude for Little Horton? You'd like that wouldn't you, honey?"

"Yes, ma'm," I said, not knowing what in the world an étude was.

Aunt Lily went to the piano and with much gesturing, played her étude. When she finished Big Mama sighed and said: "It's lovely, perfectly lovely. As fine as anything Chopin ever wrote."

"Oh, Mama, come on," Aunt Lily demurely protested.

"I mean every word of it, Sister," Big Mama said emphatically, and I'm sure she did, for she worshiped her daughter.

Much later, when I was first in New York, my aunt, desperate for recognition, sent me a number of her classical compositions, wondering if I could find some way to get the attention of a publishing house. I didn't know how, but I did meet a professor of music, German born, to whom I showed Lily's compositions. He said she was not untalented, but sentimentality had crippled what talent she had.

Chapter 13

My grandmother Cleveland lived in a two-story green frame house on McGowen Street in Houston. Streetcar tracks ran in front of her house and on the corner was a drugstore. Across the street was St. Paul's Methodist Church and next to that, a large brick mansion where my grandmother Cleveland said lived a distant cousin of my grandmother Brooks. As a girl, according to Big Mama, the cousin had been poor as a church mouse, but having married a very rich man was now a terrible snob.

My grandmother Cleveland often took me downtown on the streetcar, where we would have lunch or go to a picture show.

On these trips she would instruct me what I should do if we ever got separated while downtown.

"Son."

"Yes, ma'm."

"I don't want to scare you, darling, but Houston, like all cities, is very wicked."

"Yes, ma'm."

"Did you ever hear of Charlie Parker?"

"No, ma'm."

"Well, he lived in Philadelphia, which is a big city too."

"Yes, ma'm."

"And one day he got kidnapped."

"Who kidnapped him?"

"The Gypsies. And the poor little thing has never been heard of since."

"How old was he when he was kidnapped?"

"About your age."

"Yes, ma'm."

"So always be on the lookout for Gypsies."

"Yes, ma'm."

I thought that over for a while and then I asked:

"How do Gypsies look?"

"They're dark complected and mean looking. If I see one in town today, I'll point him out to you."

"Yes, ma'm."

"I don't know which are worse, Gypsies or white slavers."

"What are white slavers?"

"Well, there are men that kidnap young girls and send them over to China."

"What for?"

"For wicked purposes."

"What kind of wicked purposes?"

"I'll tell you when you are older, Sonny."

"Big Mama?"

"Yes, darling?"

"Are there really Gypsies in Houston?"

"They're everywhere. Oh, you have to be careful in Houston, honey. Last month I was sitting on my porch and this tramp came up to this porch."

"Was he a Gypsy?"

"No, darling. Just a tramp. And his arm was all bandaged and he said to me, lady, my bandage is coming loose. Would you be kind enough to retie it for me? I can't manage by myself. Why certainly, son, I said, and he came up on the porch and I reached out to help with the bandage, and he tried to grab me, but I was too quick for him and I jumped up and ran into the house and locked the door."

As I got older Aunt Lily would take me aside, and swearing me to secrecy, begin to tell me how unhappy she was, that neither her husband nor her son understood her because of her artistic nature. She said she loved them both and that they were good men, but she had nothing in common with them. She felt close to me, she said, because I had a more sensitive nature and should have been her son.

Once in a great while she and her husband, Uncle Will, would come to visit us in Wharton, always without warning. I'm sure if they had called first, my father would have thought of an excuse not to see them, because he obviously cared for neither of them.

The Depression hadn't officially begun in those days, but cotton prices were at an all-time low, and my father's business always seemed to depend on the price of cotton.

Uncle Will, on the other hand, was obviously prospering, and he and Aunt Lily were always dressed in expensive clothes and drove a Packard car. He worked for a Houston wholesale grocery firm and was a born salesman. He would start his visits by naming the new products his company had for sale, extolling the virtues of each. To him they were always the best without question. Then he would turn to Aunt Lily and say: "Mud, tell them how much your new shoes cost."

Aunt Lily would pretend to be embarrassed and would say demurely, "Oh, Daddy."

"Tell 'em, Mud."

Then she would shyly let us know, and it always seemed astronomical to my frugal parents. Then he would point out the window and say: "See our new Packard? Tell 'em what that set me back, Mud."

And so it would go—a long list of what they had acquired since their last visit and what it cost.

Then he would start on Houston, its virtues and its future, always implying, it seemed to me, that only fools like my father would stay trapped in this kind of small town. Then he would announce, as if we hadn't heard it many times, why he had left the Democratic party and become a Republican.

My father always became visibly depressed and withdrawn after these visits.

Uncle Will came to a sad end. His beloved wholesale grocery company fired him when he was in his early sixties, and he soon after suffered a heart attack. Two years earlier their son, Bill, thirty-seven, who worked for an electronics company in Georgia, went to a lake in Florida one afternoon, and though he couldn't swim, walked into the deep water until he drowned.

Part V

Albert Clinton Horton, my great-great-grandfather. Born in Georgia, he came to Texas in the 1830s.

Chapter 14

The Texas Colorado River begins at Austin, and winds its way to the gulf, passing through Wharton just a block and a half from the courthouse and half a block from a residential area.

My great-aunt Loula's house, now a Mexican restaurant, was only a half block away from the river, and the houses of my great-aunt Lida and my great-aunt Reenie, both torn down now, were only a little farther from the river. One of my earliest memories was hearing: "Did you look at the river today?" The replies varied. Sometimes they would report it as "low," other times as "normal," others as "pretty high." But when they answered, "It is rising fast," there was cause for alarm. People in town would go often to the river to see how high it really was and how near to submerging the river bridge, always a sign of great danger, because if the river spilled over its banks into the town and the surrounding farms, it could cause much damage.

The flood of 1913 was the one my father talked about the most. It was the flood when the Colorado, the Brazos (in neighboring Fort Bend County), the Bernard and Peach Creek all flooded, the water covering everything from Wharton to Richmond, thirty miles away. It was a vast lake, my father said, of floating livestock, household belongings, provisions and debris. Conditions were particularly bad between Wharton and the small farming town of Hungerford. Many black families were forced onto housetops and trees to save their lives.

I have some memory of the flood of 1922, for although our house was four blocks from the river, the water came into our yard and up to the edge of the front porch. Our house had purposely been built high off the ground to keep flood waters from ever entering the house itself. My mother and father kept me inside the house, because the water in many places in our yard was over my head.

The 1925 flood was, for me, a time of great drama and excitement. There was the period of wondering, would the river go over its banks or wouldn't it, and if it did, how much damage would it do? I remember half hoping the flood would happen so I could in the future talk about it as my parents talked of the floods they had lived through.

Growing up, I was never allowed to go near the river, and was constantly told tales of its dangerous suck holes, which supposedly could without warning seize the strongest swimmers and pull them under, drowning them. I remember, too, often hearing the tolling of a bell, or the wail of a fire siren, announcing that someone had drowned in the river.

When my father was a boy and lived with his grandparents, he spent a great deal of every day fishing or swimming in the river. I was always full of questions about that part of his life.

"Who taught you to swim?" I would ask.

"I taught myself."

"How?"

"I don't know, Son. I just did. I just began swimming one day."

"But it's different now, honey," my mother would quickly add. "We don't ever want you ever near that river now."

"Why?"

"Because it's different now. There are suck holes . . . and . . ."

"Weren't there suck holes then?"

"Yes," my father said. "But I didn't know it."

"Didn't it worry your mother or your grandparents that you went to the river?"

"No, they never paid too much attention to anything I did or didn't do."

I had been warned that there were alligators and poisonous snakes in abundance at the river, and so I often asked my father about that too.

"Were there alligators there when you were a boy?"

"Lots of them."

"Were you scared of them?"

"No. I didn't pay any attention to them. If you didn't bother them, they didn't bother you."

"How about snakes?"

"All kinds, moccasins, rattlers, copperheads."

"Weren't you scared of them?"

"No, if you didn't bother them, they wouldn't bother you."

"What if you stepped on one without knowing it?"

"Well, you don't do that. Look where you're walking. I always did."

"Anybody get drowned in the river when you were a boy?" I asked.

"Not that I remember," he said.

"Well, they did," my mother said.

"I don't remember, hon," my father answered. "They may have, but I don't remember."

"They were drowned down there, hon, all the time. And still are. The river is very dangerous and we don't want you to ever go near it, do we, hon?"

"No," my father agreed. "I think you shouldn't."

"Did your mama or your grandparents know you went down there?" I asked.

"Yes. Grandpa came down once and said, can you swim? And I said, yessir, and he said, let me see you, and so I showed him and he said, all right, and he went on back home."

"His mother and his grandparents let your daddy run wild," my mother said.

"My grandmother and grandfather were kind to me just the same."

"They never gave you anything for Christmas, though," I said.

"How do you know that?" my father asked.

"Mother told me."

"They gave me what they could," my father said. "We were poor, Son. I'd get an orange or an apple for Christmas and you'd a thought I'd been given a million dollars I was so tickled."

"Did they ever whip you?" I asked.

"My grandfather did," my father said. "He caught me chewing tobacco once and he whipped me real hard."

"Did you ever build a raft down at the river to go sailing on like in *Huckleberry Finn*?"

"No. All I ever did down there was fish and swim."

"How am I going to learn to swim if I can't go in the river? There's no other place to swim here."

"Well, you'll learn one day," my mother said.

"How?"

"Maybe they'll build a swimming pool here," my mother said. "To keep kids from going to the river."

"Bubs Armstrong goes down there all the time. He can swim already."

"Well, I don't want you ever to go down there," my mother said. "Your father was just lucky as a boy," my mother continued.

"I was, I suppose," my father said. "But I can't lie. I did love it down there."

My mother prevailed. I never went near the river without one of my parents, and I never learned to swim either.

I continued to fantasize about the river, though, and in my imagination it would become the Mississippi, and I would build me a raft and sail up and down and have glorious adventures like Huck and Jim.

Chapter 15

Ten miles east of Wharton is the village of Iago, and several miles beyond that is the town of Boling. Both were outgrowths of the Taylor brothers' plantation, established in Wharton County in 1871. The Taylor brothers raised cotton, sugarcane, corn, cattle and hogs and at one time had three hundred blacks working for them.

On a fourteen-mile hike to complete some phase of becoming a Boy Scout, I stopped in a country store near Iago for a bottle of soda water. On the gallery of the store was an elderly black man, and as I drank my soda water we got to talking. When I told him my name, he said he had been born a slave on my great-great-grandfather's plantation. I have never forgotten the impact that made on me. Slavery, up until that time, had been an abstract statistic in other people's stories: "Our family had one hundred sixty slaves, or one hundred twenty . . ." "We were good to them," "We never mistreated them." But as I looked into that man's tired, sorrowful face, I was shocked to realize that this abstraction, spoken of so lightly, was a living, suffering human being. The tales of the past bore a new reality after that.

Some fifty years later I was visiting my close friends the theater director Joseph Anthony and his wife, Perry, in Truro, Massachusetts, and Perry asked me if I knew of a Colonel Horton from Texas and I said yes, he was my great-great-grandfather. Perry said she had a book containing letters from slaves and two of the letters were from a woman slave on his plantations writing to her daughter.

I made copies of the letters:

Wharton (Texas), March 8, 1859

My Dear Daughter

I have written you twice, but I hav not yet received an answer from you. I can not imagin why you do not writ. I feel very much troubel. I fear you hav not received my letters or you would hav written. I sent to my little grand children a ring also a button in my first letter. I want you to writ to me on recept of this letter, whether you hav ever received the letters and presents or not. I said in my letter to you that Col. Horton would let you have me for 1000 dol. or a woman that could fill my place. I think you could get one cheaper where you are than to pay him the money. I am anxios to hav you to make this trade. You have no idea what my feelings are. I hav not spent one happy moment since I received your kind letter. I was more than rejoyest to hear from you my Dear child; but my feelings on this subject are in Expressible. In regard to your Brother John Col. Horton is willing for you to hav him for a boy fifteen years old or fifteen hundred dol. I think that 1000 dollars is too much for me. You must writ very kind to Col Horton and try to Get me for less money. I think you can change his Price by writing Kindly to him. I think you can soften his heart and he will let you hav me for less than he has offered me to you for.

You Brother John sends his love to you and 100 kisses to your little son. Kiss my Dear little children 100 times for me particuler Elizabeth. Say to her that she must writ to her grand mar often. I want you to hav your ambrotype taken also also your children and send them to me. I would giv this world to see you and my sweet little children; may God bless you my Dear child and protect you in my prayer.

Your affectionate mother,
Elizabeth Ramsey

Matagorda (Texas), April 21, 1860

Dear Daughter:

I received your kind & affectionate letter, & was glad to hear that you was well, & getting along very well. I was sorry to learn that you were disappointed in raising the amount of money required to purchase me. In a conversation with my master he says he is willing to take a woman in exchange for me, of my age, and capasity or he will under the circumstances take nine hundred dollars in cash for me. He also says money cannot buy John. He is a training John to take charge of one of his Plantations & will not part with him untel death parts them. I should be very happy to see you My Dear Daughter as well as my Grandchildren. I hope there will be a way provided for us to meet on earth once more before we die. Cant you come and see us Your Brother John is well and desires to be very kindly remem-

bered to you. Farewell Dear Daughter. May God protect
you from All evil, is the prayer of your affectionate Mother.

Elizabeth Ramsey

There was a footnote in the book on the outcome of the letter:

With the help of abolitionists in Ohio and elsewhere the
daughter was able to raise nine hundred dollars and purchase her mother's freedom. In eighteen sixty Elizabeth
Ramsey at last met her grandchildren.

After reading the letters and the footnote I went off by myself
and tried to imagine what kind of a man my great-great-
grandfather was. He left no letters or journals of any kind, or if he
did they are all destroyed. Except for his will and the scant oral
history still being passed down in my family and these two letters
from a former slave, I know nothing of him. I don't judge him,
really, but I also can't understand how a man—a deeply religious
man from all accounts, who built a church with a balcony for his
slaves, who was one of the founders of Baylor University, a Baptist college—could be so insensitive to other human beings that
he was willing to buy and sell them. I tried to imagine, for the
hundredth time, what it was like to live in that time, a white
family, surrounded by and dependent on a hundred and seventy
black slaves. This wasn't the romantic idyll of the storybook leg-
ends, I'm sure of that. In any event, that way of life was all over
five years after Elizabeth Ramsey wrote her second letter, and I
wonder what happened to Brother John, whom Colonel Horton
was training to take charge of one of his plantations.

Chapter 16

Floyd's Lane or Boling and Iago had a gin and a general store to serve the neighboring plantations and not much else until 1925, when oil was discovered and Boling became a typical boom town.

When sulphur, too, was discovered a few miles away in 1928, Texas Gulf Sulphur dug mines and built a town to house the mine workers. It was named "New" Gulf (because Texas Gulf had a plant called "Old Gulf" at Gulf Hill in Matagorda County), and what was once barren pasture became overnight a town with five hundred houses, a hospital, churches, a public library and recreational facilities.

The discovery of oil and sulphur in the county changed the lives of many of my relatives and in some ways the life of the town.

Before the major oil fields in the county were discovered, oil leases were made with a number of farms in the area. My grandfather before his death signed several of them. These individual leases were mainly for small pieces of land and though no one became rich from them, they did provide a welcome addition to the regular farm income.

A prominent doctor in town was the first to make a great fortune from the leases by going to black farm owners in areas the oil companies were interested in leasing and getting them to sign over their mineral rights to him for a small fraction of what they would have gotten if they'd dealt directly with the oil companies. The doctor bragged openly about his deceit and when I heard about it I went to my father to ask if it was true, as the doctor was a man of wit and good humor, much loved and respected in town. I'd often been told the story of what he'd said to my grandmother, when I was two or so, and she called him in a panic one morning to tell him I had swallowed a nickel and what should she do about it? "Depends on how bad you need to get the nickel back," he answered. All the boys and girls in town loved him, too, the white ones, at least, because whenever you met him in front of Outlar's Drugstore, he would call you over and give you a nickel or a dime. How, I thought, could this kind, generous man openly cheat ignorant people, many of whom couldn't read or write, and didn't even know what they were signing?

"Well," my father said, "you better learn now that some people, good people it would seem, don't mind taking advantage of poor, ignorant Negroes. To them, Negroes have no feelings, no sense, and wouldn't know how to take care of the money if they got it."

"That's terrible, Daddy."

"Of course it's terrible."

"Could you do something like that?"

"No, not if I was starving and my wife and children were starving. I couldn't."

And I believed that was so, because my father spent a great

deal of his life helping black people who couldn't read or write figure out forms and legal documents, for which he got no kind of payment, except the loyalty and affection of the whole black community, most of whom addressed him in the plural as Mr. Footes, and who on a Saturday would wait in line at his store, sometimes as long as an hour, to have him personally wait on them.

In 1933, oil and its fortunes came close to touching our family. When it was decided I was to be sent to dramatic school in Pasadena, in order to get the money for my tuition, my bus fare and whatever money I needed for board and room while attending school, my father had to sell the rental property he had bought from my mother's father in the prosperous days of World War One. He sold it for fifteen hundred dollars, and was about to send in a deposit for my tuition in Pasadena, when Louie Worthing, a close friend, came to tell him of an oil pool he was part of that was leasing a piece of land they felt reasonably sure had real oil potential. There was room for one more investor and he had come to my father to offer him a chance to participate. He would have to invest fifteen hundred dollars, and Louie didn't want to press him, he said, because it was a calculated risk, but he did feel it was almost a sure thing.

My mother told me later that my father agonized over what to do all that night, and decided finally he couldn't risk my tuition money and told his friend he had decided not to go along. I knew nothing of this until many years later. It turned out that there was oil on the land and all the investors made a great deal of money.

Unlike the doctor and his schemes, many of our friends and

relatives came by their oil leases honestly. And while they mainly didn't get rich, if their land holdings were large enough, they certainly did benefit.

People that had been struggling all through the twenties just to pay their taxes, or repay bank loans they had taken to start up that year's crop, suddenly could afford to paint and repair their houses and replace their old worn-out cars.

There were also the tales of sudden riches descending on uneducated dirt farmers who had always been just a step ahead of losing their land. Some handled it well, some didn't.

Mr. Banker and Mr. Abendroth were two of these dirt farmers. Both had farms in the Iago-Boling region and both because of sulphur found on their land became enormously wealthy, moving their families into Wharton after their change of fortune. The Abendroths had a number of children, the Bankers three, and two of the Abendroth children, Farmer and Willa Mae, and all three of the Banker children, Irene, Vivien and Bill, entered the Wharton schools. Willa Mae Abendroth and Vivien Banker were both in my class.

I was told that Mr. Banker when he got his money went to my cousin Gautier Brooks at Wharton Bank and Trust Company and asked for his help and advice. My cousin, a very conservative man, advised him well and Mr. Banker used his new money wisely and profitably. Mr. Abendroth sought no such advice. He bought cars for himself and each of his children, and people used to ride by to see these cars (all expensive) parked in the yard under the chinaberry trees of their rented house. Eventually there was a rumor that he had been taken by unscrupulous land speculators from the Texas Valley, who got him to invest huge sums of money, sight unseen, and when he did finally go to look at the land he found a great deal of it under water and unusable. However it happened, his fortune was all gone within a few years and soon after he had to get a job as night watchman of the town. I used to see him in town making his rounds all times of night. He didn't seem bitter over his quick change of fortune, nor did the children I knew. They were always amiable and pleasant and never mentioned the loss of money at all.

My father always used Mr. Banker as an example of good sense and how admirable it was not to let sudden wealth turn your head, and he never seemed jealous at all over Mr. Banker's sudden good fortune or the good fortune of his friends and relatives. Nevertheless, as I think back now, with cotton selling for so little, business in town so slow and the Depression coming on fast, those years must have been anxious times for him, particularly with his oldest son asking to be sent to a dramatic school. He must have wondered why he had missed out on all of his friends' sudden riches, and whether he was doing the right thing by letting me have my way, especially since he was being cautioned on all sides in subtle ways not to. Once my uncle Albert came to my father's store while I was there and beckoned my father to the back and I watched as they discussed whatever they were discussing, in whispers so low I couldn't hear. They talked for half an hour or so, until my uncle left, chewing, as was his custom, on an unlit cigar, saying, "You're a fool and you'll never have a dime."

And my father only answering, when he was safely out of earshot, "That may be, but what I have I'll never gamble away like you."

I asked my father what the talk was about, but he wouldn't

tell me. Later when I asked my mother she said: "Uncle Albert came, as he said, representing his side of the family, who were concerned about our letting a seventeen-year-old boy do a foolish thing like going to a dramatic school. That it would come to nothing and you would be back in a year or so, having wasted all that money, clerking in the store with your father."

He used as an example a cousin who had been sent to Princeton to study art and was now back seeing to the family farms.

If my great-aunts agreed with him, they never made it apparent to me, but always seemed supportive of whatever I wanted to do.

Chapter 17

It wasn't until my sophomore year in high school, when the speech teacher, Eppie Murphree, arrived, that I found anything in school to really interest me. Until then I took all the required subjects, but I would be hard put to tell you who taught me what or any specifics about the classes. I remember in one English class, though (I think I was a sophomore), being assigned to write a paper on the poet Keats. I took it seriously enough to read some of his poems and a great deal about his life. Whatever the merits of the paper I turned in, it was my own doing. The teacher, Miss Maureen Cummings, didn't think much of it and gave me a very poor mark. Ted Hotchkiss, the Methodist minister's son, got the highest mark in the class. He told me later that I was a fool to take the route I did, that he had read none of the poems but had simply gone to the encyclopedia and with a few changes copied what was there.

With a few exceptions, such as my Keats paper, I managed to make mostly A's and B's, although in math I was always dangerously near failing. My parents were unconcerned about my poor showing in math, putting it all on the fact that no one in our family had a math mind, and it was something you either had or you hadn't.

My parents were very calm and relaxed about all my school grades. They never asked if I was doing my homework or studying for upcoming tests. I never went to them for help in my studies or to be coached, and they in turn never offered help, unlike the parents of some of my friends, who studied with them, coached them constantly and were very ambitious and demanding about their grades.

My father, who had only gone to the sixth grade, probably couldn't have helped me if he had wanted to, but my mother, who had been salutatorian in her high school graduating class and had gone to Kidd Key College, could have.

Early on I became an insatiable reader. *Miss Minerva and William Greenhill* (a staple in those days for any Southern boy) was an early favorite, followed by a total immersion into the worlds of the Rover Boys, the Motor Boys and Tom Swift.

When I was nine or so I memorized Eugene Field's "Little Boy Blue" for a school function of some kind, and after I learned it and performed it, I would recite it to myself over and over and once in a while I would be asked to recite it again for family or friends, sometimes crying as I got to the end of the poem. Then my aunt Laura, if she were around, would always add, "You see, I told you he was tender-hearted."

We were exposed to very little poetry in our school. The only things I remember being assigned were the opening stanzas of Chaucer's *Canterbury Tales,* the whole of *Julius Caesar* and John Greenleaf Whittier's *Snow-Bound.* The Keats I read on my own preparing for my essay on the poet. Surely there must have been others, but if there were, I've forgotten them.

We had more exposure to plays than to poetry. In the third grade one of the teachers, Charlotte Garrett, presented, for some charity or other, an abbreviated version of *A Midsummer Night's Dream*, and I was cast as Puck. It was given at night in the backyard of the Garrett home. Neither my mother or father came and I expect now that the reason for their absence was that Mother was pregnant with my brother John Speed, because in those days pregnant ladies still stayed close to home. In a picture taken on my grandparents' front porch of my aunt Laura's wedding party, my mother is conspicuously absent. Since Aunt Laura's marriage took place at about the same time as my Shakespeare debut, I'm sure her pregnancy was also why my mother chose not to be in the wedding party and picture.

When I was a sophomore, and all of twelve, I was allowed to join both the Book-of-the-Month Club and the Literary Guild. Among the books sent by Book-of-the-Month were: Sigrid Undset's *Kristin Lavransdatter,* the Jalna books, Galsworthy's *The Forsyte Saga,* Willa Cather's *Shadows on the Rock, Death Comes for the Archbishop, The Professor's House* and *My Ántonia* and Vicki Baum's *Grand Hotel.* From the Literary Guild came Manuel Komroff's *Coronet,* Cellini's *Autobiography,* and *The London Omnibus,* a collection of poems, stories, essays and one play by contemporary English writers. Here I read for the first time Noël Coward's *Private Lives,* Virginia Woolf's essay "Mr. Bennett and Mrs. Brown" and Somerset Maugham's "Rain," as well as a story by Arnold Bennett. (I had already read his novel *The Old Wives' Tale.*) I also began to read Dickens and Thackeray, and Cousin Rosa McCamley, seventy-five, and a great reader herself, gave me a copy of George Bernard Shaw's *The Devil's Disciple* and Edwin Arlington Robinson's collected poems. I had earlier read and reread many times *Tom Sawyer* and *Huckleberry Finn.* As I think back now it was Willa Cather and Mark Twain that made the greatest and most enduring impression on me. I have read them both, frequently, even today.

The book clubs also sent me the collected poems of Walt Whitman, a volume of poems by Dorothy Parker and another by Edna St. Vincent Millay.

I read them all, and I wish I could say that I memorized poems in the Whitman volume, or the Keats or the Robinson, but I can't. The only two poems I remember memorizing are Dorothy Parker's and Edna St. Vincent Millay's, both of which I can recite to this day:

> *Men seldom make passes*
> *At girls who wear glasses.*

And

> *My candle burns at both ends;*
>   *It will not last the night;*
> *But ah, my foes, and oh, my friends—*
>   *It gives a lovely light!*

I used to recite these to my friends at school to impress them, I'm sure, with my sophistication and worldliness.

It wasn't until my early twenties that I began to read poetry with any seriousness. It then became a real passion.

My parents showed little interest in what or how much I was reading, unlike my father's mother, who constantly worried that I was going to turn into a bookworm like my great-uncle Robedaux Foote, who would read only Greek and Latin and, according to her, never did a useful day's work in his life.

One of my mother's friends, Anna Giles, who knew I belonged to the Literary Guild, and who was also a member, called one day to say she thought Mother should know that the guild had just sent its members Voltaire's *Candide,* and she didn't think it was the kind of book a young boy should be reading. Mother repeated to me what Mrs. Giles said, but she didn't ask me not to read it.

I was told often in later years that my grandfather Brooks was very learned and a great reader, and he would be pleased at my interest in reading, but I never remember seeing him read, or reading to me. And all I remember seeing my grandmother read was the Bible.

Part VI

The Brooks family on the porch after the house was remodeled.
Seated (left to right): *Papa (holding Tom Brooks Foote), Baboo,*
Speed Brooks, Billy Brooks, Laura Brooks with Horton Foote, Jr.;
standing (left to right): *Tom Harry Brooks, Jr.; Rosa Brooks;*
Hallie and Horton Foote, Sr.

Chapter 18

On the fifth of March, 1925, my grandfather Brooks died. I was nine years old.

A few days earlier he had been examined by a doctor for an increase in life insurance and it was discovered that he had a weak heart, and was turned down by the insurance company. He didn't tell any of this to his family.

He was taking a walk past Jack Crawford's filling station, at the far end of the downtown business section, when he collapsed on the sidewalk. He was dead by the time Dr. Davidson, the family doctor, could reach him. This was shortly after one o'clock in the afternoon. My grandmother was called, of course, and all the children then in Wharton were found and told the news. My uncle Billy, fifteen, and the youngest son, was still in high school and he was sent for immediately. I, however, was told nothing and when school was dismissed took my usual route home past the Santa Fe tracks down Burleson Street, past the Crawford house and the Baptist church and down my dirt road (unnamed at the time) to our house.

The day was a typical March Texas day, fair, not too hot, with a slight breeze from the gulf. I ran into the yard when I reached our house and went directly inside. I remember an eerie feeling as I entered, because of the quiet. My mother and my brothers were usually there to greet me in some fashion, but when I came in the front door there was not a sound of greeting from anyone. I walked through the house calling my mother's name, but there was no answer. Usually, under such circumstances, I would head out the backyard and go directly to my grandmother's, expecting to find my mother there, but for some reason I didn't and I went back out to the front yard and crossed the street to the Joplins' house. Before I could call for my friend Edwin to come out to play with me, his mother, Miss Ida, appeared and said, "Son, I think you'd better go on over to your grandmother's." I must have sensed something urgent in her voice and frightening, too, because I asked no questions, but went back across the street to our yard. Instead of going directly to my grandmother's, I went back inside our house, called my mother's name again and when I got no answer went out to our back porch where I could see my grandmother's yard and porch. I stood for a moment looking over there and all seemed normal enough to me, so I assumed the fear Miss Ida's laconic request had started in me was unfounded, and I walked out into the backyard and slowly began to cross our yard to the backyard of my grandparents. When I got through the gate separating the two yards, I saw Eliza, the cook, standing there with her sister Sarah. I walked over to them and they were talking and didn't notice me. Eliza was telling Sarah that she had felt sad and heavy-hearted that morning, not wanting to get out of bed, and when she had finally dressed and started for the kitchen to get breakfast for the family she saw on the roof of the house two doves, and she said she knew then, doves being the symbol of death, that someone in that house would die today. Before she said whether her prophecy had been fulfilled or not, she saw me and she said she thought I should go on into the house and find my mother. I remember wanting to ask her why, but being almost afraid to, and before I could ask the question my mother appeared at the back screen door of my grandparents' house and called me. She was wearing a dark dress, the kind of formal dress she usually saved for Sundays or special occasions, and that puzzled me, and as I headed toward her I saw she was crying and when I got to her on the steps she embraced me and began to sob and she said, "Son, whatever will we do now?" I wanted to ask about what, but didn't, and I stood there as she held me and continued crying. She said then I think your grandmother will want to see you, not telling me why. We went into the back porch of the house and into the back hall. I could hear the murmur of many voices as we entered the back hall and then when we went into the front hall I could see into the living room, which was filled with people, men and women, all dressed as for church, talking in quiet, subdued tones, some crying, some comforting those that were crying. I followed my mother through the front hall, to the door of my grandparents' bedroom. The door to the bedroom was closed and Mother opened it and said, "Mama, Little Horton is here." I looked in the room, and saw my grandmother crying, and beside her on a cot was the body of my grandfather. No one said he was dead. I had never seen a dead person before, but I knew, without being told, that he was. I went over to my grandmother and she took me into her arms and in between her sobs she told me how much my grandfather had loved me and how proud he was of me.

Whatever happened next, how I got out of the room, where I

went, I don't remember. I do remember my father staying home from the store, though, and my not going to school for several days.

The afternoon of the funeral my father's mother, Grandmother Cleveland, came from Houston to stay with us and she arrived early in the morning with my great-aunt Lida. I was not allowed to go to the funeral—why, I don't know—and I sat on our front porch as the funeral procession passed by a half block away down Alabama Street to the Methodist church.

I remember my great-aunt and my grandmother Cleveland talking in hushed tones about what a fine and good man my grandfather was. My aunt Lida said that when her husband died in 1918 in the flu epidemic, he had been buying a farm on time from my grandfather, and that after his sudden and unexpected death she went to my grandfather, to say that she would have to turn the farm back to him, as she couldn't afford the monthly payments any longer. My grandfather had discouraged her from doing so, and arranged payments that she could easily manage. They spoke of his many charities and how many people he helped financially and how he would never, ever be forgotten.

There was much talk like that in the days following his death. The local papers carried a laudatory editorial:

AN APPRECIATION OF TOM BROOKS

This city mourns the passing of her first citizen. I say first, because Tom Brooks was easily first in the hearts of his countrymen. Admired, respected and loved by an entire community—truly that is a fitting epitaph for any man.

A man of keenest intellectual endowments, of ripened judgement, an affability of disposition, and a saving sense of humor, he combined in greater degree than any other I have known, those qualities which go to make up a perfect citizen.

Engaging in politics in its broader phases from a sense of duty as a citizen, I always found him in his political activities, high-minded, sincere, fair and tolerant.

Few men possessed his public spirit. Combining high ideals with a sound practical judgement, his counsel was an important asset to the community and his leadership an indicia of success.

He dispensed charity unostentatiously, and no worthy cause made its appeal to him in vain.

Devoted to his family and to his state, he exemplified the truest qualities of good citizenship.

Springing from the chivalric environs of the Old South, he was true to her best tradition.

His place will not be filled in our community life in this generation.

All the stores in the town had closed out of respect for him the day of his funeral, which was the largest funeral the town had ever seen. For days after there were cards, letters and phone calls praising him and saying he would never be forgotten. There was talk of a monument on the courthouse lawn and a street being named for him. None of that happened.

My grandfather had loaned money to a great many people, and sold land that the purchasers often paid out in installments. He kept very haphazard books, with most of his transactions being done on a handshake and a verbal promise.

My twenty-three-year-old uncle Thomas Harry, whom I

called Uncle Brother, was put in charge, after his father's death, of collecting money that was owed him, but a number of the people who my family knew owed money claimed to have paid off their debts. Since there was no written proof, there was nothing anyone could do. Like the loans, talk of street naming and the monument was soon forgotten, and a few years later, the mayor sent a crew to cut down the ancient pecan tree that stood in the center of the dirt road running in front of our house, which my grandfather had given to the city with the understanding (again verbal) that the tree would never be cut down.

My grandmother was so absorbed in her grief that she paid little attention to all of this and my mother, though hurt, never dwelt on it. It made a great and lasting impression on me, though. Here was a man genuinely loved and admired in his lifetime, praised extravagantly at his death, and yet six months after he was gone, it seemed he was forgotten just like anyone else. When his name would come up through the years, usually someone would add that he was a fine man, much admired, or wonder how could such a fine man have sons who turned out so badly. Now, seventy-four years after his death, he is as unknown and unremembered as his wastrel sons. The building that housed his office in town was torn down for a bank parking lot, the house where he raised his children has been sold and the quiet street that was in front of the house began, soon after his death, its slow but steady descent into a metaphor for all the ugly, trashy highways that scar a great deal of small-town America.

Until my grandfather's death, life seemed to me just magic. I never felt so secure in my life as sitting on the porch swing of my grandparents' house, knowing I was the grandson of one of the richest families in the county and of the most respected man in town.

Back then, death had no reality for me. I was aware of course that my father's father was dead. But how or when his father died I was never told, nor was it ever discussed what had happened to his father's people. The Footes were all vague blurs to me.

I knew, too, that my mother often spoke of her grandmother Brooks (it was her house in the picture each family owned), but never spoke of her grandfather. When I questioned her about this, she said, "I never knew him; he died when your grandfather was only five." That worried me. My father's father had died when he was ten, and my grandfather's father died when he was five. I wondered if my own father would die when I was ten.

My mother often told me how her grandmother Speed, a few years dead, had come to her in her sleep and said, "Hallie, go see to your grandfather." My mother woke up then and went to her grandfather's room to find him dead.

Then, too, I kept hearing of this lady in white that appeared at various times to relatives of my father's at Louisiana Texas Patience Horton Irvin's house. When she appeared, I was told, she would start combing her long blond hair. I would never spend the night at my great-aunt's house for fear she might appear to me; and sometimes in my own house, I was afraid to go to sleep for fear someone dead might appear and tell me that my father or one of my still living grandparents had died. Still, death didn't really seem real until it took my grandfather Brooks.

My grandmother Brooks visited her husband's grave every day, often taking me with her. She would stay for an hour or so tend-ing flowers on the grave or just sitting. The only other two graves in the plot were those of her two little girls, Jenny and Daisy. I had never heard their names mentioned, and when I got home, I asked my mother endless questions about them. They were her sisters, she said, Jenny born a year after my mother, and Daisy the sixth of my grandmother's eight children. Jenny had died before reaching a year, and Daisy was only two years old at the time of her death. Jenny had died the day my aunt Laura was born. Until I asked about the two little girls, no one ever talked about them, and there were no pictures of them anywhere. And this puzzled me greatly.

Often when I was with my grandmother at the graveyard, I would wander among the other graves and see how many of them had lambs on their tombstones, to indicate children who had died in infancy. I would also notice tombstones with the names of people my family often spoke about, or people who were relatives of our living friends. I was particularly taken by a bust that the father of one of my cousins had placed beside her grave, on which he had inscribed: "I love her as I do my God."

Chapter 19

Nineteen twenty-five was a rainy spring, a time of sadness for the Brookses. I would often see my mother crying, and my father, saddened too, trying to comfort her.

My aunt Laura, married now and living in Dallas, was pregnant with her first child when Papa died. She stayed on in Wharton for a month, until the birth of her child, a boy she named Tom Brooks after her father.

Aunt Laura in her sophomore year in high school had been sent away to a girls' school in San Antonio, and after finishing there to Sullins in Virginia. After graduating from Sullins she came back to Wharton and started a kindergarten using the sun parlor of the Brooks house for her classroom. Her full name was Laura Lee and she was named for Papa's youngest sister. Everyone said she had inherited her sweet singing voice from the aunt she was named for. She was gentle and shy by nature, and I thought very beautiful. She had a scar across her throat that she said made her very self-conscious. It was the result of having swallowed carbolic acid as a baby, left within her reach by a careless nurse.

Laura's husband, Oliver Ray, had come to Wharton from Alabama when he was a boy. His father, a successful planter in Alabama, had been attracted to Texas by the richness of the soil, the moderate climate and the long growing season. He felt it was an ideal place to raise potatoes. His first year in Wharton the weather conditions were ideal and he made a large crop. The next year he was almost as successful. But the following year the rains started early and continued for weeks until the potatoes rotted in the ground. It was so the next year and the next, and in despair he gave up potatoes and tried farming cotton. Again, the weather was against him and crop after crop failed.

Oliver's grandfather Asa Ray had come to Texas at the same time as his son and his family, and had started a store out in the country. He was alone there one night when a young black man came in and shot and killed him, all for a can of sardines, which was the only thing he took. Embittered by this and by the constant crop failures, the Rays sold their farm and moved to Dallas.

A year after moving there, Mr. Ray had a flat tire on his way home one night, and when he got out to change the tire was struck down by a passing motorist. He was dead by the time he could be gotten to a hospital.

Oliver and Laura had been going together for some time before the Rays moved, and they became engaged just before he left for Dallas with his family. After several years passed and they still hadn't married, Laura's family began to wonder if they ever would.

Laura finally gave him an ultimatum, I was told, and plans for a wedding were soon being made in spite of his small salary (he was night clerk in the Dallas post office).

They were married in the spring of 1924 in my grandparents' living room.

After the birth of her son, when Laura returned to Dallas, my grandmother gave them the money to build and furnish a house, and also found other ways to help them financially without wounding Oliver's pride. They had two more children, a boy and a girl.

Seven years after my grandfather's death, when I spent the year of 1932–33 in Dallas before going to the Pasadena Playhouse, I visited often in their home, and though now I realize how difficult it must have been to have to manage on his post office salary, I never had any sense of that when visiting them. Aunt Laura never had help, as my mother did, but she was always cheerful, loving and welcoming.

My grandmother had rented a house in the Dallas suburb of Oak Cliff during that time, and I was living with her, my uncle Speed and my uncle Billy. Billy, after flunking out of the University of Texas his freshman year, was going to night law school in Dallas and Speed was as always looking for work, which as usual he never found. Whenever I was alone with Aunt Laura she would begin on "the boys" and what was to become of them.

Once that year, I went into Aunt Laura and Uncle Oliver's bedroom for something or other, and saw on the table beside their bed a book called *How to Become an Executive.* Uncle Oliver had been reading it, I'm sure, looking for a way out of the night shift of the post office. He never managed to leave, staying on until after my grandmother Brooks died and left Aunt Laura a share of her estate. He retired soon after that and they left Dallas for Aransas Pass on the gulf. They lived there for a number of years, until he became ill. They moved back to Wharton then, living in an apartment where he died. She lived on there with her youngest son until, in her nineties, she died.

Chapter 20

After my grandfather's death, I spent a great deal of the spring of 1925 with my grandmother, going there when I got out of school and often spending the night with her.

I loved being in my grandmother's home. There was always a sense of abundance there. My father, always so frugal, worried about the size of her grocery bills and her other expenses. She often served three different meats for dinner and supper, because Billy, Speed or Brother didn't care for one or another of them. And in spite of her grief, she continued to entertain many of the town's lost souls, particularly widows, to whom, because of her own loss, she was increasingly sensitive. She also continued entertaining the elders of her church, and the Methodist preachers who came to Wharton to hold revival meetings, and once a year she gave a supper in honor of the current high school teachers.

My mother came to one of the suppers for the teachers, in the early fall of that year, attending without my father, because he preferred to work in his garden that night. On such occasions it was my job to stand by his side, holding a lantern so he could see what he was doing.

The Brooks boys, too, were having supper with the teachers,

and after the meal was over my uncle Brother got his pistol and said he was going to shoot out back toward the garden to see how my father, who was a known coward when it came to guns of any kind, would react.

I was holding the lantern and my father was silently working away when the pistol was fired in our direction. My father, terrified, yelled: "Drop the lantern, Son, and run. They're trying to kill us."

Drop the lantern I did and we both ran in a panic to the safety of our back porch. My mother, her two other brothers, my grandmother and all the teachers had gathered on my grandmother's back porch to watch as my uncle shot the pistol.

After we reached the safety of our back porch and the pistol shots had ceased, we could hear everybody laughing as they crossed over to our backyard to share the joke with us. My father pretended to find it amusing that he had been so fooled, but I could tell he was really furious and had to force himself to be gracious.

My father had a horror for guns of any kind. When he was growing up in Wharton it was a time when most men and some women carried their guns with them whenever they left home. It was a time when public hangings were still held at the courthouse yard and people came from all over the county to watch, a time when black men could be lynched, when there were knife fights among drunken gamblers in the saloons and when political and family feuds often ended in death. One of the most famous and long-lasting feuds came about after Reconstruction when some of the white men of the county formed their White Man's Union. My father often tried to explain to me about the two factions at odds over the forming of the union, one called Woodpeckers and the other Jaybirds, but I could never get it all straight. I do remember that there were a number of deaths because of this feud.

One of my father's stories about the violence of the time concerned a black man who was caught stealing cattle. As punishment his captors sewed him inside the carcass of one of the stolen cattle.

As a boy, my father said, he was in terror of some of the men he had to pass on the street, because he knew they had killed and would kill again and were said to get pleasure from it. He was as afraid of knives as he was of guns, citing again and again what happened to that friend of his who'd gone to a dance in the neighboring town of El Campo, only to have his throat cut by some of the local boys who resented his being there.

Chapter 21

The Brooks boys, Thomas Harry (called Brother), John Speed (called Speed) and William Smith (called Billy), were twenty-three, twenty-one and fifteen at the time of their father's death.

As the troubled and troubling sons of an affluent family, Brother, Speed and Billy were, in many respects, representative of a whole social class in the rapidly changing economic structure of the American South during the first quarter of the twentieth century.

My grandfather, besides loaning money and buying and selling land, owned a number of farms, all of which were farmed by tenants or sharecroppers. Neither he nor his sons ever went near the land except to inspect what the tenants were doing. Very few families of their day and class in Wharton lived on the land, and even those that did never worked it or farmed it, but used tenants to do all the work. Unless you were a doctor, a lawyer or a merchant, there was no work for a young man to do in Wharton in those days. The doctors were all near starving, and the lawyers weren't doing much better. The wealthier families sent their sons to college, and if the young men came back to Wharton to live, they would maybe go out into the countryside twice a week, like their fathers before them, to see how the tenants were doing on their farms. They thought of themselves as rich boys but most of them really weren't. They had many acres of land, but the crops—cotton, corn and sugarcane—they grew were no longer profitable, certainly not enough to support their ever-increasing dependents. To keep up their scale of living the land was mortgaged and year after year what little profit there was from the crops went to pay off these mortgages. The young men of these families were often indolent, and arrogant, and many of them became drunkards or compulsive gamblers.

Brother and Speed both began drinking at an early age and did poorly in school, and so at fourteen and twelve they were sent to Allen Academy, a military school, where boys of similar background with behavior or academic problems were sent in the hope they would be, as my grandmother often put it, "straightened out." Brother and Speed weren't. They kept on drinking and they began gambling, too, particularly Speed, who became great chums with the Lee boys, whose father was a rich Houston oil magnate.

Somehow they both managed to graduate from Allen Academy, Brother first and then Speed. After graduating Brother was sent to Texas A&M, where my grandfather had gone on a scholarship and graduated with honors. But unlike his father, Brother made poor grades and was on the verge of failing when he got a local girl pregnant and was expelled in his sophomore year. He came back to Wharton and went to work at T. Gordon's dry goods store. Mr. Gordon, a Jew, was a great favorite in town, and one of its leading merchants. He had three daughters, the second of whom, Annette, was considered very beautiful. I don't remember ever seeing her, but I do remember being told often of her beauty and of my uncle's infatuation, and of how deeply he was affected when she suddenly died. I remember, too, his coming home with my father on Saturday nights after their respective stores were closed, when my mother would have supper waiting for them. After they ate she would play the songs that my father had brought with him when they married and my father and my uncle would sing as she played.

After Annette's death Brother began going with my father's first cousin, Mabel Horton, who was another beauty. She was a senior in high school when they began their courtship, and for the first time the school had a yearbook, and a contest to elect a beauty queen. The winner's picture was to be put in the yearbook. The beauty queen was to be decided not by popular vote, but by bought votes. I remember the contest and how involved the whole town was in who would win. I kept hoping my uncle Brother would outspend everyone, but he didn't, and Mabel lost. She was certainly the most beautiful and most of the town was disappointed that she didn't win. Everyone thought she and my uncle would marry, but he stopped seeing her soon after, and she went to Houston to work. After a while he began going to Houston regularly to see another girl, at least that's what his family thought, but he never said so himself. Six months later he stopped his trips to Houston and seemed very depressed, and it was assumed that the girl, whoever she was, had jilted him. I remember going over to my grandmother's and seeing him in the living room sitting by the phonograph listening to sentimental songs of the day and looking very sad.

"He's grieving, Son," Mother said when I asked her about this.

"What's he grieving about?"

"I don't really know. We think he was in love with a girl in Houston and she jilted him."

"Did you know the girl?"

"No. He's never even mentioned her name."

"Why didn't you ask him?"

"Because I didn't want to know."

"Why?"

"Because we all think she wasn't the kind of girl that he would want his family to know, or he would have told us about her."

"What about Mabel? I thought they were in love. Did she jilt him too?"

"No. The other way around."

"He jilted her?"

"Yes."

"Why did he do that?"

"I don't know. Maybe he met this other girl in Houston and liked her better."

"But Mabel is so beautiful."

"I know."

"She should have won the beauty contest."

"I know."

"Do you think he'll ever start going with Mabel again?"

"I don't know. I doubt it. She's living in Houston now."

In the meantime Mabel in Houston married William Chamberlin from Mississippi. They were married only ten days when he accidentally shot and killed himself. We read about it in the *Houston Chronicle* the next day:

Ten days ago Mrs. W.F. Chamberlin, 22, of 1420 Sul Ross, and her 25-year-old husband rode west together on their honeymoon.

Both were extremely happy.

The girl was dressed in white.

Saturday night the two rode east—their last ride together—the bride in a Pullman car stricken with grief and her young husband in the baggage coach ahead. She was dressed in black.

He led her to the altar in Trinity Episcopal Church on January 25. Now she is taking him to his old home in West Point, Mississippi, to the grave.

The accidental discharge of a pistol, which he raised jokingly to his head, apparently thinking it was unloaded, Friday night killed W.F. Chamberlin, 25, cotton classer for Williams, Inman and Company, while his bride looked on.

The shot was fired at their home at 11:20 p.m. Forty minutes later physicians at St. Joseph Infirmary pronounced the man dead.

Just fifteen minutes before the tragedy occurred, Mrs. P.E. Cleveland, of 710 McGowen, aunt of the girl, called the two by telephone. Mrs. Cleveland told the story.

Auntie, I'm so happy, the girl told her. I'm just afraid it won't last.

We're the happiest persons in the world, the young husband joined in.

Then the two told Mrs. Cleveland about a wedding present some friend had given them that night. They had just opened it.

And Saturday both the aunt and the girl were blaming themselves for the death of Mr. Chamberlin.

They were over here the other day, Mrs. Cleveland said. I asked William why he didn't buy a gun and leave it with Mabel. You know there have been several burglaries in their neighborhood lately and they had some silver and jewelry.

So the boy bought a gun, but forgot to take it out of the car Friday afternoon when he came home from work.

I thought you bought a gun, his wife said.

Oh, I forgot, he said. It's in the car, and he got it.

He held it up and I looked at it, the wife said. It's a pretty thing, I told him, and handed it back.

It was bedtime and I turned my back to turn out the gas stove.

Mabel, if I thought you didn't love me, I'd shoot myself, he said jokingly, and just then I heard the gun go off.

I looked around just as he fell to the floor, and a big stream of blood was pouring from his temple.

Neighbors in the apartment next door said they heard the two laughing and talking just before the shot was fired. They heard the shot and thud of the body as it slipped to the floor.

The wife rushed upstairs to the apartment of Mrs. T.H. Spencer, where friends were playing cards.

He shot himself.

She screamed as she went: He shot himself. He shot himself. He shot himself, Mrs. Spencer said. That is all she could say.

The neighbors rushed into the room. The boy was in a pool of blood, and blood was flowing from a wound in the temple.

All night long sleep refused to come to the eyes of Mrs. Chamberlin. Saturday morning she could not sleep.

I was so happy, she said. . . . Now he's gone.

The girl's father, A.C. Horton of Wharton, called a physician who put her to sleep at noon.

She's all unstrung, the father said. It seems like she's had more than her share of bad luck. She lost her mother in 1918, and her aunt, who had been a second mother, died not so long ago. Now her husband is dead. She thought so much of him, too. It will nearly kill her.

Saturday the bridal apartment at 1420 Sul Ross was locked.

The body was sent to West Point, Mississippi, for burial by the Houston Undertaking Company Saturday night. Mr. Horton and his daughter, Mrs. P.E. Cleveland and a married sister of the girl accompanied the body to Mississippi.

There were rumors in town that she was still in love with my uncle Brother and her husband knew it and that's why he killed himself, but our family didn't believe that and insisted it was an accident. Mabel returned to Wharton. She wore black and looked even more beautiful than ever. Brother in the meantime had gone to Arizona with a friend to work on a cotton ranch, and he returned from Arizona in the fall of that year.

I'm not sure exactly when I became aware that my parents and my grandparents were concerned and anxious about the boys, as they continued to call them.

I knew that my aunt Rosa, only two years older, used to coach her brother Tom in the evenings since he was doing poorly in school, and I remember there was much discussion, little of which I understood at the time, about sending Tom and Speed, two years younger, off to Allen Academy.

Billy was six when his brothers went off to Allen Academy and he seemed headed for a normal small-town existence, doing well enough in school, playing football and taking part in other sports. He and a neighborhood girl, Frances Wright, were selected king and queen of some celebration or other and he played the saxophone and with a group of other boys formed a small dance band, playing, I remember, at several Valentine's Day and Washington's Birthday teas sponsored by the Methodist Ladies. I began to go to the town dances when I was thirteen and it was then I became aware that Billy was drinking, too, but since most of the boys his age were drinking at the dances it didn't seem strange to me, and if my grandmother knew about it she didn't seem concerned, and always talked of his becoming a lawyer like his uncle Billy, for whom he had been named.

Indeed at this time I didn't see anything unusual in the behavior of any of my uncles. I was around Brother and Speed only when they were at my grandmother's house, and if they were drinking then, they took good care to cover it up. It was from remarks I would hear from my parents and aunts and people in town (never my grandparents) that I gradually began to realize that there were signs of real trouble for my two oldest uncles. I remember once when a cousin, Nannie Mae Brooks, was visiting my mother and I heard her say, "Tom is always such a gentleman even when he is drunk." I heard my mother repeat the remark later to my father, saying she felt it was very insensitive of her cousin to have said something like that, and my father not answering her, but shaking his head and sighing.

"Don't you think it's insensitive, hon?" My mother insisted on an answer.

"I sure do, hon. Every day some old reprobate finds a way to come by the store to say, I saw old Tom last night. He sure was drunk. He was just roaring drunk, or, I saw Speed over at Little Bobby's last night. He lost a lot of money. It's a good thing he's got a rich Mama."

Later it was only Speed who drank in my presence. I was the most fond of Speed of all my uncles, and I knew he was fond of me. He was a wit and could always make me laugh. For a while he ran a cleaning and pressing shop, and sometimes he would take me for a ride in the evening in his delivery truck. He'd tell me the gossip of the town, who was getting drunk and who had lost money gambling. He usually had a flask of whiskey somewhere in the truck and he'd take it out from time to time and have a swig. He never asked me not to tell anyone he was drinking, but I never did, nor did he ever offer me a drink. He was an enigma to the family. He never dated a girl that anyone ever knew of and when his best friend, Bolton Outlar, got married to our cousin Nannie Bennett and wanted him to be best man he refused and wouldn't even go the wedding. And yet I knew that he went across the tracks to the black prostitutes with his other friends. He never mentioned sex to me or offered to take me across the tracks to introduce me to the prostitutes like some of his friends did for their younger brothers and nephews, but he let me know that he went by telling me stories like the one of the wealthy planter who was in love with a beautiful mulatto prostitute who had jilted him for a white gambler from Galveston, and whose love letters the prostitute would read when drunk to the white boys visiting her whorehouse.

He was the first of the Brooks boys to get into serious trouble, when one night he went to a neighboring town with some of his cronies. They were all drunk and went to a dance where one of his friends got into an argument with a local boy over a local girl, which led to a fight, and the Wharton boy took a car jack and hit the local boy on the head, killing him. There was a terrible commotion then and Speed and the three other Wharton boys, including the one that had struck the blow, were all arrested and taken to the local jail. There was a trial and Speed, of course, had to testify not only to the drunkenness of his friends, but to his own. His friend was acquitted and came back to Wharton a free man. The rumor was that it cost the father of the boy fifty thousand dollars to have it turn out so. My family hoped that this tragedy would stop Speed's destructive behavior, and it did for a while, and soon after he got a job at a wholesale grocery that my grandmother had bought stock in. That didn't last long, though, and then he and my grandmother decided he should open a cleaning and pressing shop. Why they decided this was a business for him, I've never known. She bought all the equipment for him and gave him free rent in a small building she owned. This lasted three years, when he walked away from it, selling the equipment at a loss to a friend. He never worked again in his life, and he lived to be sixty-three, sustained by the cash handouts given to him by his mother.

After my grandfather's death my grandmother was faced with the decision of who was to manage the farms and invest the money he left her. There was also the necessity of collecting on loans he had made to a number of people in town. My grandmother decided finally to let the Guardian Trust Company in Houston invest the money, and let Brother take over managing the farms and collecting the loans. My aunt Rosa had begun this process, but she was anxious to finish her master's degree at Columbia University, so she left again after two months for New York City.

My grandmother asked my parents what they thought about turning the farm management and the collection of debts over to my uncle Brother. Both said they felt it must be her decision, but privately they were concerned.

Brother began to go into Houston to see Mabel, now a young widow, and soon after he and Mabel got married, and he brought her back to Wharton to live. He was having difficulty collecting on the loans my grandfather had made, and also felt the job demeaning, so with the consent of my grandmother it was turned over to someone else. He then got a job in New Gulf, which was the newly established town, where they had just begun the mining of sulphur. I don't remember what he did for the sulphur company, but the job didn't last long, and next he announced he was going to run for the office of county clerk. My grandfather had been elected county treasurer for many years and my great-uncle Peter Gautier had served even longer as county clerk.

My grandmother, in the meantime, decided to deed one of the farms to him, hoping, as she said, to encourage his behaving responsibly now that he was married. She also built him a house and bought him a car. I would often see him and Mabel riding around town together. She would be snuggled up as close to him as she could, and they both seemed very happy.

My father was not impressed by any such signs of happiness. They are living way beyond their means, he would tell me. Then he would caution me not to tell my mother that he said this, as he didn't want to worry her.

"Has he stopped drinking?" I asked.

"I don't think so. He was in the store the other day and I could smell it on him."

"Is he getting drunk?"

"No. I can't say he is doing that, but he is going around asking people for votes and if I can smell liquor on his breath, they surely can."

"Maybe he doesn't drink when he goes asking for votes."

"Oh, yes, he does. I can't tell you the number of men that have come in here to let me know they could smell liquor on him when he came asking for votes. But for God sakes don't mention this to your mother. It would just upset her for nothing."

"Where is he getting the money for his campaign?"

"From your grandmother. Where they all get everything. She thinks she's helping them by giving them money no matter what, but she's ruining them. Utterly ruining them."

I changed the subject. I couldn't bear to hear any criticism of my grandmother. I thought she was perfect. Finally, I had to try to defend her.

"Well, she's only doing what she thinks is best," I said.

"Well, it's not best and never has been and never will be. They're going to ruin her, you know. She's going to wind up in the poorhouse."

That terrified me. The idea of my grandmother ending up in the poorhouse.

"Why don't you talk to her, Daddy?"

"About what?"

"About the boys."

"No. It's none of my business at all."

I didn't sleep that night, picturing my grandmother in the poorhouse, the sheriff selling her house to pay her debts.

My mother and father, while not defending Brother, also blamed Mabel. They felt she was extravagant and insisted on living way beyond their means. In any case, it was always my grandmother who paid. Their house had been given them by my grandmother and was furnished handsomely and expensively by her.

My father still felt, however, they should not give advice, and though he and my mother discussed Brother almost every night, they never mentioned their concerns to my grandmother.

The county elections were held on a Saturday and a blackboard was put up in front of one of the drugstores and at nine o'clock after the polls closed a county official would write the returns on the blackboard as they came in from the towns around the county. My daddy, since it was Saturday, had to stay in his store and couldn't watch the returns with the rest of us, but my grandmother had Speed drive her, my mother and me to town early on so we could get a good parking space in front of the drugstore. From the beginning it was obvious Brother was not going to win. We watched for half an hour or more, when my grandmother, her face sad and drawn, said, "Speed, take us home."

Brother began drinking heavily after that. Even I could tell when I met him that he was often half drunk. Mabel began to complain. She had her older sister, Willa, call on my grandmother and ask her to help. She told my grandmother that Brother went to bed drunk every night, and asked her to talk to him. She did but to no avail.

Mabel got pregnant and had a boy, named for Brother, and even my skeptical father hoped fatherhood would make Brother sober up. It didn't, and I was in my room one night when I heard my grandmother come in through the back door calling my father's name. He was on the front porch with my mother and I came onto our back porch to tell her where they were. I could tell she was very upset. I went back to my room and she joined my parents on the front porch. She was crying and very distressed. She kept saying over and over, "What have I done wrong. My God what have I done wrong."

Then I heard my mother say, "What's wrong, Mama?"

And my grandmother sobbing, unable to answer at first, and then saying, "Your uncle Peter Gautier came to me today and said that Brother has mortgaged the farm I gave him, and that the bank, since he's defaulted on all his payments, is being forced to foreclose, and that your brother had come in again today to mortgage his house and he was drunk when he came in."

"He can't do that," my father said then, "not in the State of Texas you can't mortgage your house."

"Surely Brother knew that, Mama," my mother said.

"Your uncle said he was so drunk, he didn't know what he was doing or saying."

My grandmother was crying again then.

"Oh, Mama, don't cry," my mother said.

"Big Horton?"

"Yes, ma'm."

"What am I to do?"

"I can't tell you what to do."

"Hallie . . ."

"Mama, I wouldn't know how to advise you."

"Well," she said after a long pause, "I can't have the farm lost. It was one of your father's favorite farms. I'll pay off the bank note and put it back in my name. Mabel complains all the time about his drinking. I haven't wanted to bother you with all that. Every time she comes to me, I have your brother come to the house and I tell him what Mabel says."

"What does he say?" my mother asked.

"He always says he's sorry and he'll quit. But, of course, he never does. I don't know what to do. Big Horton, what shall I do?"

"I can't advise you about something like that."

My grandmother had begun suffering from asthma, and her worst attacks often came during a crisis with one of her sons.

She did pay off the mortgage on the farm and put it back in her name.

Mabel and Brother separated and he moved in with his mother and brothers, all three boys home now. He didn't stop drinking, and my grandmother's attacks of asthma increased. I was with her one day when she was in bed resting from one of her attacks. Around five o'clock in the afternoon Brother came in. He was obviously drunk, and he was trying to hide it. He looked terrible, tired and very dissipated. I got up and gave him my seat beside my grandmother's bed. He didn't speak. He took her hand and held it.

Finally he turned to me and asked: "How are you gettin'
along, Son?"

"Pretty good, Brother."

"Pretty good? How about very good?"

I couldn't wait to get out of the room. My grandmother
looked so weak and vulnerable and my uncle so pitiful and
defeated.

He left town soon after that. He went to Galveston and got
work on a boat doing I never knew what.

Mabel divorced him and got to keep the house. After my
grandmother left Wharton for good to move to Houston, she
offered her house to my mother and father. My father thanked
her, but said he was content with the house she and Papa had
given them. He told me privately, however, that he wouldn't
take her house because he knew the boys would feel free to come
back at any time and put up with him.

Billy left Wharton with my grandmother and lived with her
off and on until she died. After Brother went to Galveston, he
only came back to Wharton once or twice. I also saw him once in
New York when the ship he was on came into port. He found out
where I was and came to see me. My aunt Rosa was in New York
City at the time and we had a visit with him for a few hours.
Brother on this last visit I ever had with him was not drunk, but
he looked terrible, wasted, and his eyes bloodshot, his hands
trembling. After he was gone I found he had left twenty dollars
behind for me, money I needed badly at the time. When I told
my aunt Rosa of his kindness to me, she said, "Well, I'm glad he
did that for you, but I wish he would do something for his own
son. He never sends money or gets in touch with him in any
way."

He died in 1950 in Arizona, where he was working picking fruit on a ranch. My mother and grandmother went to Phoenix for the body and brought it back to Wharton. He was buried beside his father in the family plot, near the graves of his two infant sisters Jenny and Daisy, and baby Johnston, Aunt Rosa's baby that was born dead. I couldn't get home for the service but I was told Mrs. Howard, a family friend, sang "In Heavenly Love Abiding," and my grandmother after said that was the hymn she wanted sung at her funeral, and it was.

Part VII

My father behind the counter in his men's store in the 1950s.

Part of Wharton's Main Street as it looked when I was a boy.

Chapter 22

My father never had a clerk to help him in his men's store, and so was never able to come home at noon for dinner. My mother finally persuaded him one summer to hire his seventeen-year-old cousin Robert Abell, that later I was to write a story for, to work for him so that he could take a midday break. Robert didn't turn out to be a happy choice. As soon as my father left the store for his house, Robert would go to the back, sit down in the swivel chair at my father's desk and have himself a nap. Once when he was sleeping away, someone came into the store and emptied two of the drawers, making off with two dozen shirts.

My father never dared leave Robert alone after that, but he kept him on as a clerk until he left for college, because he didn't want to cause hard feelings, as he said, in the family.

The following summer when I was twelve I began to take soup to my father every day at noon, waiting around while he attended to a few chores outside. I was not allowed to wait on customers if one came in, but only to tell them that my father would be back soon and to ask them politely to have a seat on the stool under the ceiling fan near the front of the store, or in a chair at the back. But above all, without having them know it, I was to watch them like a hawk, so there would be no further incidents like the shirt stealing when Robert was the clerk.

When I was thirteen my father hired me as a part-time clerk coming to work after school weekdays, and all day Saturdays. The Saturdays were long and often tedious, beginning at eight in the morning and not ending until eleven or twelve at night, depending on business.

Saturday was our big day, if there was to be a big day, and particularly so during cotton season, when the farmers and the farmhands would have money to spend.

The wagons, the trucks and the cars would begin arriving in town on Saturdays soon after nine o'clock. There would be a small trickle at first, gradually increasing until by three or four in the afternoon (depending on the weather), the sidewalks would be so crowded with country people, black and white, that it was almost impossible to make your way through the crowds. Then, added to all this, beginning usually at five, the town people would begin to arrive, some on foot, others bringing their cars and parking along the main street to watch the crowds from the country. Even in winter when cash was scarce with most of the country people, there was a carnival atmosphere almost every Saturday. The country people were dressed in their best and most colorful clothes, and even if they had no money to buy anything of substance, they always had enough to buy a hamburger or soda water. They would visit with each other standing on the sidewalks, laughing and talking like it was some gala holiday. I loved to stand in the front of the store those days listening to their talk, their laughter, their teasing of each other. I knew many of them by name and they would call out greetings to me as they passed by our store. Nearly always on Saturday in the late afternoon Dr. McCann, the black dentist, and his wife would come into the store. They were a handsome couple, barely black at all, but almost white, and stylishly dressed. My father always insisted on waiting on them himself but once in a while when the store was filled with country customers waiting in line to have my father serve them, he would apologetically turn Dr. McCann and his wife over to me. And that always pleased me, because I was fascinated by the two of them, so handsome and elegant. I wanted to ask them many questions. How did they get to Wharton? Why did they stay? Where did they live? Across the tracks with the other black people? Were they rich? Today I wonder how they stood all the restrictions of segregation. Of course, I never asked them any of those questions, and if they felt put upon in any way they never let on. They were always courteous and gracious. After they had made their purchases from me, my father, always wearing a measuring tape around his neck on Saturdays, would leave whatever customer he was waiting on and come over and shake hands with them and thank them for coming.

The other black professional in town was Dr. Martin, a physician. He never came into the store on Saturdays, but only on weekdays. He was a Wharton native and he and my father had known each other all their lives and were about the same age. He was a quiet, gentle and unassuming man and was, my father always said after he left the store, a credit to his race.

I think my father brought me into the store at such an early age so he could keep a watchful eye on me, and teach me, as he said, the value of a dollar, and I'm sure to try in any way that he could to keep me from becoming like the Brooks boys.

One day I was sitting under the ceiling fan in front of the store when he called me from the back and said he wanted to have a talk with me. He was at his desk going over some invoices when I joined him.

"Son," he said very solemnly.

"Yessir."

"I talked it over with your mother and I've decided to open a charge account for you at the drugstore."

"Yessir."

"I know you'll treat such a responsibility wisely, and not abuse the privilege."

"Yessir. I certainly will."

"Well, that's all I wanted to tell you. You can go on back up front now."

"Yessir. Thank you, Daddy."

"That's all right, Son."

I walked back to the front of the store feeling very proud that my father had such confidence in me, and I wish I could say I didn't violate that confidence, but I can't, for not only did I begin almost immediately going to the soda fountain at the drugstore where I had the charge account and buying Cokes and milk shakes for myself, but I began treating all my friends too.

It was compulsive and I knew it, but I couldn't somehow stop. I knew, too, that the bill for all this was mushrooming and that on the first of the month, Mr. Jay Terry, the owner of the drugstore, would bring the bill to my father to be paid and my folly would be discovered. Still I couldn't stop myself, and finally on the day before the first I began to pray that somehow it hadn't happened, or that I was mistaken in my fears and the amount spent wasn't as large as I imagined, or that Mr. Terry would vanish off the face of the earth, taking my debt with him. The first of the month arrived and I was in the store, racked with anxiety, but the day passed and Mr. Terry didn't appear. I was visibly relieved, and took it somehow as an omen that I would be spared. But my euphoria didn't last long, for early the next morning Mr. Terry appeared and I saw him hand my father a sheet of paper and my father turn white, looking at it.

Mr. Terry left and my father called me to the back of the store. He showed me the bill. I had charged twenty-eight dollars for drinks, a great deal for that day and time, when Coca-Colas were a nickel and a dime could buy the most expensive sodas.

"Son, have you lost your mind?" he exploded. "Do you want to bankrupt me? I don't think you're ready to handle this kind of responsibility, Son."

"Yessir," I said, mumbling, "I guess not."

One of my jobs in the summertime was bill collection. The first of every month I was given ten or so statements to take personally to the men owing my father money. I was instructed to give them the bill politely and if they said they couldn't pay then, to ask, still politely, when I could expect them to pay. I was never good at the last part, but it didn't matter, because usually after glancing at the bill as if they had never seen it before, although I had by this time in most cases presented the same bill six or seven times, they would invariably say come back on the fifteenth or the twentieth, I'll have something for you then. They never did, of course, and I would say to my father what good does it all do? They'll never pay. But he didn't agree and so month after month I would have to make the same weary pilgrimage.

One of the men my father insisted I visit each month was

"Dearie" Burtner, who had been my scoutmaster when I was a Cub Scout. All the boys in town called him "Dearie," which was what his wife called him. A large, affable man, he worked at the cotton gin, which was quite a walk from our store, particularly in the summer heat. You never knew just when he would be in his office at the cotton gin, so sometimes I would have to make the trip five or six times before finding him in. Some men were rude when I gave them their bills (usually for small amounts—ten, fifteen or at the most twenty dollars), but never Dearie. He always greeted me warmly with, "Hello, son."

"Hello, Dearie."

"It's hot out there, isn't it, son?"

"Yessir, burning up."

"Well, sit down and rest."

"Thank you."

"Do you miss the Scouts?"

"Yessir."

"I do too. You know the old Dennis house we had our meetings in? They're tearing it down."

"My heavens," I would say.

"Isn't that terrible. One of the oldest houses around."

"Yessir."

"How are your mother and daddy?"

"They're fine. Thank you."

"Tell them hello for me."

"I will, sir."

"Do you have a bill there for me?"

"Yessir."

"I tell you, why don't you come back at the fifteenth of the month and I'll have something for you then."

"Yessir, thank you, I will."

"Why doesn't he pay the bill?" I would ask my father. "It's only twelve dollars."

"Because he doesn't have it."

"Why? He works at the cotton gin."

"I know. Poor devil. He has an extravagant wife. They owe everybody in town. She'll keep him strapped till he's in his grave."

My father finally gave up on Dearie and I didn't have to go back anymore, which was a great relief to me. I would meet him once in a while uptown and he'd stop me and say he missed seeing me and was I well, and I'd say I was fine and once he asked me to come have a Coke with him and I went with him to the drugstore, and I noticed he paid cash for the Cokes.

My father was always giving me not so subtle lectures on men that lived within their means and those that didn't. He had plentiful examples in Wharton for both cases.

When I finished my two years in Pasadena, I had gotten a job of sorts at a summer theater in Martha's Vineyard and I was going on from there to New York. He called me into the store and with great solemnity he gave me fifty dollars and said, "This is all I'm ever going to give you. When this is spent, don't ever come back to me for another dime, because I won't give it to you."

When I tell this story to my children, they ask, "Do you think he meant it?"

"I guess I did, because I never did ask him ever again for money. Not even when I sometimes went hungry, and he never gave me money again except fifty dollars when I got married and fifty dollars when each of you children were born."

* * *

The store I worked in for my father was the third space he had occupied since going into business for himself. I don't remember the interior of the first or second building although I know where both were. The first was a narrow building, half the width of the store where I worked. The second, a larger space, was now leased by Butler and Grimes, a chain store that sold toys and household goods. My father's third store was rented from the Kellys, an old Wharton family. Mr. Kelly, a lawyer, had his offices above the store and nearby was his house, a huge white two-storied affair, with a wide gallery in front, where he often sat in the late afternoons or evenings. Between our store and the Kelly house was a small building, also belonging to the Kellys, which housed a dry goods store owned by the Kreitsteins, a Jewish family, who, unlike most other Jewish merchants in our town, had not prospered. Rarely did I see a customer in their store, and their merchandise seemed, even to my untrained eyes, shabby and unattractive. Mr. Kreitstein and his wife, Hannah, were usually seated on stools in the front of their store and would wave as people passed by. Mrs. Kreitstein in particular was a friendly soul, and was always most sympathetic to families in trouble. She cried frequently as she talked and would recount to you in great detail all the sad and tragic events suffered by various families in town. My grandfather Brooks had in some way befriended the Kreitsteins when they first came to Wharton and they never failed to express their gratitude to him, telling me over and over what a fine man he was and how sad it was he had to die. They had one child, Bertha, who had, as my parents said, been raised on the streets, a jolly, friendly soul, who learned to talk in Wharton, and had a broad Southern accent, almost as if she had learned to speak a black dialect. Her parents had a strange way of speaking, with traces of a Southern accent mixed with their Yiddish accent. The Kreitsteins had been brought to Wharton, I was told, by Joe Schwartz, Mrs. Kreitstein's brother. Mr. Schwartz at the time had a dry goods store and was the town's most prosperous merchant. I often wondered at the disparity in the fortunes of the two families and when I questioned my father he said there was no explaining it, and when I asked how Mr. Kreitstein managed to stay in business, he said it was a mystery to him, and when I wondered what would happen to them if his business failed, he said they would be taken care of by the other Jews, who, unlike the Gentiles, were always loyal to each other and ready to help out. I believed that for the longest time, until I witnessed the same rivalries and jealousies among the Wharton Jews as among other ethnic groups, and had my observations verified, in time, by the tales of Abe Davis.

Abe was a nephew of the Schwartzes who also had been brought to Wharton by Joe Schwartz from Boston, as I remember. Abe had no New England accent when I knew him, but one of the thickest Southern country accents I've ever heard. And he had adopted all of the town's and region's prejudices with a vengeance. He would appear in my father's store at least four times a day, chewing on an unlit cigar, often bragging about the business he was doing or expected to do in his own store. My father had a great affection for Abe, but would shake his head after he left and tell me to believe only half of what he said. Abe had come to Wharton to clerk for the Schwartzes, and did so until it became known that Mr. Dave Dickson, then the owner of a store called the Hub, wanted to sell it. Abe bought him out and opened a dry goods store himself. How he got the money to do so, we never knew, but my father always surmised that Mr. Schwartz had loaned him the money. All this had taken place before I went to work regularly for my father. Abe called my father Al or Foote and he was one of the first people I remember doing so. Most of the Brookses called him Big Horton and me Little Horton. His aunts all called him Sonny. The blacks always called him Mr. Footes, or Mr. Horton. The sign in front of his store said, "Al. H. Foote. Men's Store."

Mr. Dickson, the Hub's former owner, was also a constant visitor to my father's store. He was very frugal, a good merchant, and had prospered. He had invested his savings in land, and now owned a great deal of it. After his retirement from the store, he spent most of his time seeing to his farms. He was a tall, wiry man at least twenty years older than my father, and unlike him in most ways, but they were devoted to each other. When my father was expanding his business from cleaning and pressing to men's furnishings, Mr. Dickson came to him and offered to loan him the money to get started. He didn't have to take his offer, but my father never forgot it. During the Depression, Mr. Dickson again came to my father and offered him money if he needed any. He was my father's closest friend in spite of the difference in their ages. Mr. Dickson was from Alabama and had married Eula Edwards, also from Alabama. They lived in a Victorian cottage, built by the Pridgen family, half a block from our house. My father and Mr. Dickson often walked home together after closing their stores and they continued to do so even after Mr. Dickson sold his. A talkative man, he spoke with great rapidity, asserting his often unconventional opinions about religion and politics. My father, usually intolerant of anyone not an avid Democrat, listened patiently to his emotional diatribes against Roosevelt and the whole of the New Deal. He was an atheist who never kept his views to himself, and if he was there when my mother visited the store, he would delight in getting her into a discussion about religion, though he was not able to shake her faith in God. My father, who had not much religious conviction of his own, never took on any of Mr. Dickson's radical beliefs, but would just listen patiently every time Mr. Dickson began his diatribe against the foolishness of religion.

On weekdays in the summer I was at the store full-time: 7:30 A.M. until 6:00 P.M. closing time. But if business was particularly slow, my father would let me leave at 4:00 or 5:00.

My father's store had two show windows on either side of its entrance. He changed the display of merchandise in the windows every month. He sold men's ties, shirts, underwear, hats, "ready-made" suits, socks, work clothes and "dress" clothes. One of his chief sources of income was his tailoring department, as he called it. "Tailor-made" clothes were particularly popular with his black customers. They would come in from the farms on a Saturday and go to the side of the store where the samples of cloth hung to see what kind of material they wanted their suit made of. If none of these samples pleased them, he would show them two large "tailoring books," which contained many small samples of suit material. Once a customer decided on the fabric for his suit and agreed on a price, my father would take a tape measure to measure him. He would check all the measurements several times and carefully write them down on an order form, all the while keeping up a lively conversation with the customer, about his crops, his friends, his wife or girlfriend and his children. The black customers mostly had to buy their clothes on time, often making a down payment as low as three dollars.

My father kept careful books recording these payments, giving the customer receipts for every dollar received. The suit or pants usually arrived long before they had finished paying for them, but the customers would be called in to try on the clothes to see if any adjustments were needed. Usually they weren't because he was meticulous in his measuring. If everyone was satisfied with the result, the suit was then put away with the customer's name on it in a huge showcase to the left of the store where all suits, ready-made and tailor-made, were kept, to be given finally to the customer when the last payment was received. On the right side of the store were the showcases for the shirts, socks and ties. He had all the merchandise carefully marked with a code telling what he paid for it and what price he was charging the customers. It was a proud day for me when he taught me this code, and showed me how to use the cash register, a large, old-fashioned affair, which made a cheerful sound when you struck its keys to ring up a sale or take money out.

In the twenties and thirties, when some of his black customers began migrating to California and Chicago, they would write him asking him to make a suit for them, knowing he kept a record of their measurements. Many of these men were almost illiterate and had never written letters before. One of his favorite letters was from an old customer now in Los Angeles, who started his letter "Mister A.H. Footes, Dearest One."

In the center of the store just as you entered was a large showcase containing hats. This was changed seasonably—for fall and winter it contained felt hats and in spring and summer, straw hats of all kinds. Several feet beyond this showcase was a table that the cash register rested on and beyond that were several tables containing work clothes: khakis, pants and shirts, overalls, striped and solid colors, piled high, since work clothes were one of his most popular items. The best dress shirts cost as little as $2.50, and he had shirts for $1.95, and a few for 95 cents. The work clothes ran $1.50 for shirts and $2.50 for the trousers and overalls. I can't remember what he asked for ties, handkerchiefs or men's jewelry (tie pins, cuff links), but I'm sure they were comparatively cheap. The hats and the ready-made and tailor-made suits were of course considerably more, but I don't remember a hat costing over $5.00, and I'm sure the price of the suits, if I could remember, would seem ridiculously low today.

Every week or so a drummer would come to call on him to see if any of his stock needed replenishing. They were usually genial, outgoing men, carrying sample cases of their wares, going from town to town to see what they could sell. My father, since he had been on the road as a salesman himself, was usually cordial to them and they would spend an hour or so answering his questions about how business was in the adjoining towns (Bay City, El Campo, Victoria, Richmond), before getting down to the business of looking over any new patterns or designs they had to offer and then placing the order for new merchandise. Usually each drummer had a specialty. The hat salesmen only handled hats, the shirt salesmen shirts and ties. The hat salesmen always came to the store with a great deal of anticipation, because usually my father bought a great many.

As my father's only clerk, my duties were well defined. I was to sweep out the store every morning, then go to the post office (there were three deliveries in those days), and to the bank if there was a deposit to be made. On the way either to or from the post office or bank I would stop at the drugstore for a Coke, usually Rugeley's, as my great-uncle by marriage owned it, and I always felt a strong sense of family loyalty that made me want to trade with any of my kin that were in business. When I returned from the post office or the bank, there was usually some pants or a suit to be altered for a customer and I would be sent to my uncle Speed's shop to get his tailor to make the needed alterations. His shop was called the Deluxe Cleaners and to get to it I went down an alley directly across from our store, passing the back entrances of a number of stores and the Plaza Hotel. Also in the alley was a small black barbecue joint that played race records on a jukebox at top volume. I had been told that at one time most of the stores had been saloons, and behind them in the alley had been a series of one-room whorehouses called cribs. I knew from my father that as a boy he had searched the alley looking for empty whiskey bottles to sell back to the saloons, and I would wonder what it had all been like then. But he never mentioned the whorehouses to me and I was too shy to ask him about them.

My uncle Speed usually called me "Hoss" and always seemed glad to see me. At the front of his shop was a counter where he received the clothes to be cleaned, pressed or altered, and behind that was a divider that shut off the public part of the shop from where the cleaning and pressing were done and the clothes alterations were made. In the wintertime the back of the shop was kept warm by the steam from the presses, but in the summer it was sweltering, so that even without their shirts, the men who worked there dripped with perspiration. He employed a white man to do the altering of clothes, and two men (usually black) to do the cleaning and pressing. Once in a while my uncle helped out with the cleaning and pressing, but more often he drove around in a small truck making pickups and deliveries to his customers. Every morning he would get in his truck and pick up clothes from people in town to be cleaned and pressed and every evening he would deliver them back again. I never knew why he decided to sell his business, but I presumed it was because he was not making any money, or he was bored. I knew he was drinking steadily at the shop, for he made no effort to hide it from me, often taking swigs from a bottle that he kept in the back of the store.

Once the shop was sold, he did nothing, wandering around town, gossiping with his friends, until he moved to Dallas with my grandmother to look for work. He came back to visit once in a while, usually staying at the house of his friend Bolton Outlar, who had married our cousin Nannie Bennett, and it was she who discovered he was not only drinking whiskey, but taking pills called red devils. From red devils he became addicted to heroin and was arrested in California when he was caught buying it and sent to the penitentiary, where he served part of his sentence and was then paroled. Buckshot Lane, the sheriff and someone he had grown up with, went to California to get him when he was paroled, as a favor to my grandmother, and brought him back to Houston, where my grandmother was living by then with her son Billy, her daughter Rosa and Rosa's little daughter, Daisy Brooks. My aunt Rosa told me later that when the drug dealers learned that he was again in Houston, they called constantly on the phone trying to make contact with him. After a year or so of finding no work in Houston he went back to California, where he was arrested again, this time for selling heroin, and he was sent to San Quentin for ten years. My grandmother died while he was in San Quentin, and when he was finally released he again came back to Houston and lived with Aunt Rosa until she died.

My aunt Rosa, born in 1900, was the aunt I was closest to. She was obviously very bright and intellectually ambitious. She graduated from the University of Texas and then went to Columbia University for her master's degree.

After graduating from Columbia she married Dick Johnston, handsome and affable, but soon after their marriage he began drinking excessively. They had a son, born dead, the first year of their marriage. Dick was unable to keep jobs and they had to go live with his family in Waelder, Texas. It was there she had her second child, a girl she named Daisy Brooks. Dick's drinking kept increasing and she felt for the sake of her daughter she had to leave him. With her baby daughter she joined my grandmother in Dallas. When my grandmother left Dallas, Aunt Rosa and her child went to Houston, where she became a social worker. Two years later, my grandmother left Wharton permanently and bought a house in Houston, where Rosa and her baby joined her. A great deal of the time Billy and Speed lived with them too. Rosa had more understanding and compassion for her brothers than anyone in the family. In a way she gave her life to them, getting them out of one scrape after another, never deserting them, no matter what they had done. She was caring for Speed and seeing to Billy until the day she died.

During the school year I only came to the store after school, except on Saturdays. We had no bathroom at the store and I would watch the store while my father went to the Hub to use the bathroom, or to the drugstore for a cup of coffee. I would sit on a small bench that was in the front of the store under a slow-moving ceiling fan. I would get bored usually after about fifteen minutes and I would go out to the sidewalk, hoping someone would pass by that I could talk to. Across the street was Schlick's hardware store, to the right of it was Stallings' meat market and grocery store, where my father traded, to the left of that was the alley leading to my uncle's shop and left of that was the Western Union office, later taken over by Millard Walker for his insurance business, and next to that was Miss Lily Frazier's hamburger stand. Miss Lily Frazier was from East Texas, and had come to Wharton with her mother and her son to be near relatives. She began her shop in the late twenties. At first it was a tiny place just big enough for a counter and grill, but her hamburgers were popular and as her business increased the size of her shop increased until she had tables and chairs where one could sit and eat. She talked as if everyone were deaf, she had a piercing laugh, and she called all blacks "niggers," often to their face (my father said that this was because she was from East Texas where they talked like that), and if she wanted to get the attention of a particular black male, she would call out, "Boy, come over here," or "Uncle" if he were an older man. On Saturdays her place would be packed with country people, black and white, buying hamburgers or soda water. I ate her hamburgers on Saturdays, too, and always brought one to the store for my father, as he preferred eating alone in the store.

Weekdays were usually very quiet in the store—if we had a customer every hour or so we would feel fortunate. My father would always wait on them, and the purchases were often small, a handkerchief or a shirt or a pair of work pants. I don't know how he survived on the small volume of business he did, and he

wouldn't have, had it not been for Saturdays and his country customers. During cotton season, beginning in July and ending in
October, when there would be lots of buying from the country
customers, my father would take care of the hats and the ready-
made and tailor-made suits and he would let me handle work
clothes, dress shirts and ties. He would greet each customer by
name as they came into the store, sometimes waiting on two
or three at the same time, or calling out cheerfully, when he felt
there were more customers than he could handle, "My son
will take care of you." Often, though, they wanted no one to wait
on them but my father and sometimes there would be as many as
ten customers waiting in line for him. Saturdays were long days,
summer or winter, spring or fall. The store was opened at seven-
thirty then and we would often stay open until eleven-thirty at
night. If business had been good my father would declare that he
could have gone on for another twelve hours; if it had been disappointing, he would end the day silent and withdrawn. But at
the end of the night, when the last customer had left and we had
straightened out the merchandise in some fashion, he would
always say, "Let's go get some food," and we would go to either
Ray's or the Manhattan Café and talk over the events of the day.
If it had been a good day he would be in a marvelous mood,
recounting the highlights, the number of hats or work clothes
sold, and questioning me about some of the customers I had
waited on, particularly about those that had left the store without buying anything. Then we would head for home, walk past
the flats, the livery stable, the blacksmith shop, the black restaurants, all closed this time of night, through the cotton fields
owned by my great-great-uncle Edwin Hawes, on across
Alabama Street to the dirt road with the huge pecan tree and

finally to our house, where my mother would be waiting to hear how our Saturday had been. If it had been a good one, he would repeat again all the happenings of the day, the sales he had made, the money taken in. If it had been a disappointing one, he would have little to say and my mother knew enough not to ask any questions.

I spent a great deal of time when I was in the store alone checking the cash register. There was a key that if you pressed it would give you the total amount put into the register that day. Often on a weekday, there would be only ten or fifteen dollars, but on Saturdays, it could be a different story; sometimes the total would be several hundred dollars. How did he make it with such a small volume of sales? I don't know, but I guess it was by saving every penny he could. Since there was no overhead except for the rent and lights (we had no telephone), and he gave me only three dollars a week, he managed to squeak by. Sometimes he didn't make it, though, and had to get loans from my great-uncle Peter Gautier Brooks, who was vice president of the bank, to get us through the year. Though I was no longer living in Wharton, I know his business increased greatly during the Second World War, and when he died he left my mother quite a comfortable estate, which he had made partly from the earnings of the store, but also from the investments he had begun to make in the stock market. He was a careful, cautious investor, read various business journals avidly and was most conservative in his choice of stocks.

On weekdays there was a steady stream of men who came into the store not to buy anything, but to talk and gossip. The first visitor was almost always Mr. Charlie Bolton, who was born in

Georgia and had come to Wharton as a young man, marrying
Jennie Olivia Watts, who was descended from an early Wharton
family. They had nine children. The oldest was a girl two years
older than my mother, the youngest a boy my age. They lived in
an enormous frame house on Richmond Road, with a yard lined
with sycamore trees. Mr. Charlie (as my father called him) usually arrived a few minutes before nine. By then I had spread the
floor with a compound I had been instructed to use before sweep-
ing, and my father had tidied up any last-minute disarray from
the night before.

There were never any formal greetings when Mr. Charlie
entered the store and walked toward the back where my father
sat at his desk, writing in the ledger where he kept careful nota-
tions of all his sales. As Mr. Charlie walked slowly down the
aisle, my father would look up to see, as if he didn't know, who
was approaching. The first words were always spoken by Mr.
Charlie. Not hello, or how are you this morning, but always an
analysis of the current weather.

"It's a nice day. I hope it continues," or "It looks like rain," or
"It's chilly this morning. I lit a fire in the stove when I got up,"
or "It's going to be a scorcher today."

My father would answer in kind, nearly always agreeing with
Mr. Charlie's assessment of the weather. This was usually followed
by an assessment of how the present weather would affect the cotton crop, followed by an assessment of the prospect for the cotton
crop, and by a summation of cotton crops in the past, during lean
years and abundant years. By this time Abe Davis, the owner of the
Hub, or Mr. Dave Dickson, its former owner, would wander in and
Mr. Dickson would add his memories of cotton crops of the past.
Abe, being a comparative newcomer to the town, would listen to

these tales of cotton crops of the past, and then my father would usually join in, often reminding his audience of 1918 when they had an abundant cotton crop and the price was an unheard-of forty cents a pound. Then they would comment on the pitiful price of cotton today, wondering if it was worth growing cotton at all, with Abe the progressive newcomer timidly suggesting that the farmers in the county should try new crops.

"In the South," my father would say with great authority, as if he were sharing a great new truth, "cotton is king." Then Lloyd Rust, whose family owned many cotton farms and was related to my family, would join them. If it were before Roosevelt was elected president, he would add his complaints about the chancy nature of cotton farming. But after Roosevelt became president he would always begin with a tirade, venomously attacking Roosevelt and the whole New Deal and most particularly his farm policies. Since he was fond of his cousin, my father usually said nothing until after Lloyd had left the store, and then he would begin to explode, saying, "What's wrong with him? Roosevelt and his farm bill saved the South and the cotton farmers."

The remaining men would agree or disagree according to their feelings about Roosevelt and the New Deal.

But one day, Lloyd's outburst of hatred for Roosevelt was too much for my father and, his anger matching his cousin's, he began vigorously defending Roosevelt and attacking his political enemies. Lloyd, startled at the passion of my father's defense, walked out of the store.

When he left I said to my father, "What's wrong with him? Surely he knew you were devoted to Roosevelt, you have an NRA poster that he looks at every day and a big picture of Roosevelt on your desk."

"He'll get over it," my father said.

"Will you apologize to him?" I asked.

"For what, for speaking the truth about our president?"

Days passed, then weeks and months, and his cousin didn't come back to the store again. I know this concerned my father, for he was devoted to his cousin, but both were too proud to apologize for their anger. It wasn't until my brother was killed in the war that they were reconciled.

By noon the visitors had one by one left to go to their homes for dinner, and in Mr. Bolton's case dinner and a nap.

"Does Mr. Bolton work, Daddy?" I asked my father.

"Yes, he's in insurance."

"Do you buy insurance from him?"

"Yes."

"Does he make enough money selling insurance to take care of his family?"

(I knew there were nine children, and although the four oldest had married, there were still six at home to be fed and clothed.)

"I guess so."

"Does he have an office?"

"In his house."

"Were those ten children ever at home at the same time?"

"Yes."

"How did they all fit in?"

"It's a big house."

"It would have to be."

In the wintertime, even on Saturdays, the men, always Mr. Dickson, and at frequent intervals Abe Davis, chewing on his cigar, and various other friends of my father's, usually those he called old-timers, would drift in and the talking would resume. After commenting on the weather and its effect on plowing or planting they would begin discussing some local or county problem. The Texas Gulf Sulphur Company had only recently discovered sulphur in our county, and there was much discussion about this giant operation whose roots were in hated Wall Street. Sometimes the arguments got personal and vicious, accusing the sulphur company of paying the county judge and certain county commissioners for tax favors. The haters of the sulphur company, mainly the old-timers, blamed them when the brick courthouse, the pride of the town, had its steeple removed, and its bricks covered over with yellow cement, making it look, they said, like a block of sulphur. Another line of conversation among the men was the arrival in town of Mr. Copenhaver. He had come to Wharton from the North, with his family, to work at Mr. Wilson's cotton gin and oil mill, and soon began, again according to the old-timers, to take over the town, beginning with a job at the Chamber of Commerce. A few of the men would say they felt Mr. Copenhaver's Yankee energy was good for our sleepy town, and then would begin the arguments about what was good or not good for Wharton. Some of the newcomers (living in Wharton only twenty-five years could still brand you as a newcomer) would often complain that the five families who had settled in Wharton before the war (Civil War) and had acquired plantations of many acres, and held on to their land, refusing to sell any of it, were keeping the town from expanding. My father usually stayed out of these arguments, but when the men had all gone and we were closing the store for the night, he would tell me, since we were related to most of the landowners, that he admired them for holding on to their land and that it was their children that worried him, because he wondered if they would know how to keep the land together. Then, swearing me to secrecy, he would often begin analyzing my uncles again, saying how they were the kind of boys (he, too, always called them boys rather than men) that could get rid of an estate overnight. Then he would voice his concerns once more about their bankrupting my grandmother and sending her to the poorhouse.

I liked it best when the gathered men would begin to reminisce about the old times, when Wharton was often lawless, filled with feuds and outsized characters, some ruthless, some generous.

Casey Clifford, one of the regulars, had a favorite story, which he would begin when one of the men would ask, "Casey. Do you know who cut down the sycamore trees around the Courthouse Square?"

"Nope."

"Come on, Casey."

"I swear to you."

"You were living here then, weren't you?"

"Oh, yes."

"And you wanted them cut down?"

"Well . . ."

"Come on, Casey."

"What happened, Casey?" another man asked.

"You were here then, you remember."

"But Leo here wasn't. Tell him what happened."

"All I know is there was a faction in town that didn't want any sycamore trees around the Courthouse Square, they felt it should be pecan trees."

"Why?" Leo asked.

"Because," Casey said, "pecan trees are native here and some people thought since it was a cash crop here in the county we should advertise the fact by having pecan trees around the courthouse, instead of sycamore trees. Both sides got quite worked up over it. And the arguments went on and on, week after week, until finally one night a group of men insisting on having pecan trees came down to the courthouse in the middle of the night and decided to settle the argument by cutting down all the sycamore trees, and that's what they did and went home to bed, and the next morning the town woke up to all the sycamore trees around the Courthouse Square cut down."

"Who cut them down?" Leo the newcomer asked.

"No one knows to this day," Casey said.

"Everybody knows," a man said. "But we just can't prove it. Casey, for one."

"Prove it," Casey said.

"You have us there, Casey," one of the men said.

"And you have to admit a pecan tree is more suitable for our courthouse than a sycamore tree."

"Well, it's done now," Mr. Dickson said. "You can't do anything about it now."

Everybody agreed that was so.

"But there was a time that tempers were flaring over those trees," Mr. Dickson said, laughing. "I thought for a time blood was going to be shed."

Casey turned to my father. "Al."

"Yessir, Casey."

"How did you feel about all that?"

"I stay out of things like that, Casey."

"Just criticize Roosevelt to him," Mr. Dickson said. "You'll get an opinion about that."

"I'm very proud of our president," my father said.

"I'd like to see how proud you're going to be when the country is bankrupt."

"Just leave Roosevelt out of this," Casey said. "Al, I bet Leo hasn't ever heard your story about the Jackson boys and Mr. Marsh."

"Oh, sure he has. I've told it a million times."

"Well, hell, tell it again. You haven't heard it, Leo, have you?"

"Sure haven't."

"Well," my father began. "The Jackson brothers used to have a farm out near Glen Flora."

"On the river?" Casey asked.

"I don't think right on the river," my father said. "But near it. And Mr. Marsh had just come here from England and he was managing the lumberyard, and the Jackson brothers got acquainted with him there."

"They were bachelors," Casey said.

"That's right," my father said. "And one day one of them came in and asked him to come out to the country and have supper with them that night, and Mr. Marsh was delighted by the invitation, and Jackson told him how to get there on horseback and asked him to be there by six. Mr. Marsh said he would be there promptly, so he closed the lumberyard early and saddled his horse and went on out to their farm about five or six miles from town. When he got there he was greeted by only one of the Jackson brothers, and Mr. Marsh said he could tell he'd been drinking, but thought nothing of it at first, and only became alarmed when he continued to drink, until he was obviously very drunk. The cook, a black woman, called them for supper and they went into the dining room. Mr. Marsh asked his host where his brother was, but he got no answer at all. Mr. Marsh sat down at the table while the cook brought in the food. He said he had never seen so much food in his life. There were six vegetables, plus rice, sweet potatoes and three large platters heaped high with fried chicken. Jackson filled Mr. Marsh's plate with the vegetables, rice and sweet potatoes and six pieces of chicken. Mr. Marsh waited for Jackson to serve himself before starting to eat and when he didn't, Mr. Marsh said, may I serve you, sir? Jackson looked at him and sneered and took a pistol he had strapped to his waist and said, I don't want any chicken. I want to watch you eat it. Begin now, God damn it. Mr. Marsh began to eat the chicken, Jackson staring at him all the time. When he had finished the vegetables, the rice, the sweet potatoes and all the chicken on his plate, he said, thank you, Mr. Jackson. It was delicious, but it's late and I think I'd better get on back to town now. He said he started to get up from the table when Jackson pointed the pistol at him and said, sit down. You ain't going no place until you eat every piece of chicken on those platters. Sir, I'm full, Mr. Marsh said. I can't eat any more chicken. You will eat it, you bastard, or I'll blow your goddamn brains out. Mr. Marsh saw he meant business, and he began to try to eat the chicken. He was on this tenth piece and feeling like he was going to die, when the cook came to the door. She must have sensed what was going on, because she asked Mr. Jackson to come into the kitchen. He did so, and Mr. Marsh said the minute he disappeared into the kitchen, he ran out of the house, jumped on his horse and rode back to town as fast as he could."

The men are all laughing by now, and my father is laughing with them.

"Mr. Marsh told me," he said as he brought his laughter under control, "he's never been able to eat chicken of any kind ever since."

Each of the men then began to tell their own stories of the past. The scandals, private or public, and the deaths by drowning in the river, the tales of gamblers, and drunks, and murderers, and the ones murdered, of adulterers and adulteresses, of when this brother did that, and no it was the other brother, hour after hour. I was reminded of all this many years later when I read Elizabeth Bishop's "The Moose."

> *In the creakings and noises,*
> *an old conversation*
> *—not concerning us,*
> *but recognizable, somewhere,*
> *back in the bus:*
> *Grandparents' voices*
>
> *uninterruptedly*
> *talking, in Eternity:*
> *names being mentioned,*
> *things cleared up finally;*
> *what he said, what she said,*
> *who got pensioned;*
>
> *deaths, deaths and sicknesses;*
> *the year he remarried;*

the year (something) happened.
She died in childbirth.
That was the son lost
when the schooner foundered.

He took to drink. Yes.
She went to the bad.
When Amos began to pray
even in the store and
finally the family had
to put him away.

"Yes . . ." that peculiar
affirmative. "Yes . . ."
A sharp, indrawn breath,
half groan, half acceptance,
that means "Life's like that,
We know it (also death)."

Sometimes standing outside the store on the sidewalk I would be visited by some of the old-timers, black and white, never talking about the present, but always about the past. One of these was Delia Davidson, an ancient black lady who had been raised from childhood by the Dr. Coon Davidson family. The Coon Davidsons had all left Wharton many years earlier, but someone of their family would usually write Delia once a month giving her their news. I had heard of the Coon Davidsons all my life, but never knew any of them, since they had left Wharton before I was born. But Delia knew I knew of them and she would stop every time she had received a letter and read it to me. Then she would ask, "You didn't know I could read as good as you, did you?"

"Why sure I did, Delia."

Then she would tell me for the hundredth time, "You remember Dr. Coon, don't you? And Miss Lily?"

Before I could answer I knew of them, but never knew them, she would say, "Clarkie died. It was so sad. It broke all our hearts. She died at sixteen. She was an angel in heaven. She was your mama's best friend."

"I knew that, Delia."

"And you want to know something else? I know my multiplication tables. Know all the books of the Bible. The Coon Davidsons raised me and taught me like one of their own."

Then she would do a little of the multiplication tables, and look at me as she paused as if she expected me to show astonishment, which I tried to do, then she would give a chuckle and say, "Bless your heart," and walk on.

Chapter 23

As I began my teens I learned to dance. I don't remember now who taught me, but by the time I was thirteen, I could waltz, fox-trot, and do a local variation known as "belly rubbing," which meant not moving but simply standing still and rhythmically rubbing your stomach against your partner's.

There were dances almost every Friday night at the Norton Opera House, a huge barn of a building with a stage at one end, which had originally been used for Chautauqua productions, plays and concerts. (It was here my father heard Chauncey Olcott sing "Hello, Central, Give Me Heaven.") It was used now only for dances. Admission was twenty-five or fifty cents, depending on how much the orchestra cost. Sometimes there were dances on Saturdays, too, but mostly on Friday nights. I always had a date—I had begun to go steady at thirteen with Martha Jay Winn and most of the boys I knew in school had dates too. Once in a while a boy or a young man came without a date, and they were called stags.

In my father's day each girl would be given a dance card, and it would be up to her date to see that he had some of his friends sign up for every dance. In my day, we had no such customs. The stags would stand in the center of the dance floor and when they saw a girl they wanted to dance with, they'd tap her on her shoulder, as she danced around the room with her partner, and say, "May I?" then her partner would release her to the "tagger," and he would go to the center until he saw a girl he wanted to tag. Some poor girls though would rarely be tagged at all and their partners would be stuck with them most of the evening, sometimes giving subtle but desperate signals to their friends to tag the girl in question and give them some relief. Why the unpopular girls would put themselves through this kind of humiliation week after week I couldn't understand.

There was one girl from a lovely family, as my great-aunt Loula would say, who wasn't conventionally attractive and never popular with boys. The girls in our class all adored her and would begin early in the week convincing the various boys who hadn't made a date for the dance to ask her. Finally, a boy would give in, and call and ask her to the dance, as if it were his own idea. It would always turn out the same. They would start the dance talking and laughing, but then as the evening wore on and no one tagged her, a sense of desperation would settle over the boy's face. The girl would try to continue to smile and keep up the conversation as they danced around the floor, the boy becoming more and more withdrawn, making desperate signals behind her back for a friend to rescue him. My father hearing all this would shake his head and say it was sad she was so plain, that she was a nice girl, then he would add, "I swear, I don't understand God sometimes."

There were all ages at the dances. Besides the high school

crowd, there were the young married couples, and the dating couples no longer in high school, and the couples in their early and mid-thirties, most of whom had been married for a number of years.

Bootleg whiskey was readily available in the town and county then and cocktail parties for the young and older couples had become the rage, so some of the couples would arrive at the dances already half drunk, and during intermission would go out to the cars to continue drinking. One of the older married women would often be so drunk when she arrived that she would just stand stationary in the middle of the dance floor the whole night incapable of any movement other than belly rubbing.

There were very few dances in the summer because of the excessive heat, and often in the spring and fall and even in the winter the temperatures would be in the eighties, and both men and women would be dripping with perspiration before the night was over. We sometimes had the black orchestra of Teddy Singleton playing for the dances, but more often it was the white orchestra of "Red" Cornelson.

Both orchestras played the same standards of the day: "Stardust," "Dream a Little Dream of Me," "I'll Get By," "Tip-Toe Through the Tulips with Me," "A Cottage for Sale," and everyone's favorite, "Tiger Rag." When that was played the crowd always insisted it be repeated time after time, the tempo increasing with each repetition.

Always at the dances were chaperones, mothers of some of the high school girls, and they stayed until the end to be sure that nothing unseemly took place, and, I'm sure, to see to it that their daughters never left the hall at intermission time.

After the dance we would take our dates to a Mexican restaurant nearby, which stayed open until the dance was over, and order enchiladas or tamales or chili and drink Cokes.

My family had no car so I was at the mercy of my friends whose parents owned one to take me and my date to the dances.

Bill Copenhaver, who had a roadster with a rumble seat, was one of these friends. After he went off to military school I double-dated (as we called it) with Stanley Moore or my cousin Robert Abell, both of whose families had cars, until they went off to college, and then I can't remember who gave me and Martha Jay transportation, but we got there somehow.

Chapter 24

My mother never learned to play bridge and never seemed to have any interest in it, nor in taking part in any of the very active and constant social life of Wharton.

She often said she didn't play bridge, or entertain in other ways, because she cared nothing for that kind of life, finding it empty and frivolous.

Almost every day, sometimes three times a day, there was a party or a tea or coffee given someplace in Wharton. My mother accepted no invitations, and never entertained. And perhaps it really was because that kind of activity didn't interest her, but I think, too, she did it out of love and consideration for my father, because he was having such a struggle to make any kind of living, and she didn't want to burden him with any extra expenses.

In time Mother's closest friend became Fannie Mae Garrett. Fannie Mae had often been in the Brooks home because of her friendship with my aunt Laura, who was in her class, and after Aunt Laura moved away to Dallas, Fannie Mae began to visit Mother.

Fannie Mae's father, John Garrett, was a Gentile, her mother,

Sophie, a German Jew. It was the only such marriage in town. John Garrett was from Florida and Sophie's family had a long Texas history. There were four Garrett children: Fannie Mae, the oldest; Aaron; Leon and Isaac. They were raised in the Jewish faith, but because Mrs. Garrett did not want her children to associate with the other Jews in Wharton, who had come from Poland or Russia, they were not allowed to attend the local synagogue and they celebrated the holidays in a Houston synagogue.

The Garrett children had only Gentile friends, and when Leon, the second son, defied his mother and married the daughter of a local Jew, his mother refused to speak to him and forbade Fannie Mae and her brothers to have anything further to do with him. The youngest son, Isaac, married a Gentile and joined the Methodist Church, and though Miss Sophie (as her children called her) didn't approve of that either, she accepted it with some grace, as did Fannie Mae and her brothers.

Fannie Mae never had a beau, or even a date, with Jew or Gentile, that we knew of. She had taken one trip away from Wharton to Victoria, Texas, sixty miles away, when she was in her twenties, and talked of it constantly as if it had happened just the week before. Aaron became a druggist, and though he never married, was involved with various Gentile women, none of whom Fannie Mae or her mother approved of, and many nights Fannie Mae would go riding around town to find out what lady's house Aaron's car was parked in front of.

After Leon and Isaac married and Mr. Garrett died, Fannie Mae and Aaron (Bubber, she called him) lived on with their mother, and devoted they were, too.

In time, Mrs. Garrett became senile and had a complete loss of memory, retreating into total silence. She was the first person I knew that this happened to.

She was finally confined to her bed and Aaron, after working all day and some nights at the drugstore (in those days all three drugstores stayed open until eleven), would come dutifully home, unless he had a date with one of his Gentile girlfriends, and lie in the bed beside his mother until it was time for him to undress and get into his own bed.

My mother and I were frequent visitors in the Garretts' Victorian cottage, built in 1880, all of cypress wood they would proudly tell you. And after Miss Sophie became bedridden, at the beginning of each visit we had to first go into her bedroom and pay our respects to her. Fannie Mae would lead us over to her mother's bed and speak to her as if she understood what was being said.

"Mama," she would announce as we approached the bed, "Hallie and Little Horton are here to see you." There would be no response of any kind from Miss Sophie, and after a few more moments of pleasantries about how well her mother looked, and indeed she did look well, physically healthier and stronger than either Fannie Mae or Aaron, we would leave Miss Sophie and go into the living room to have Fannie Mae catch us up on the latest Wharton news.

She was a witty conversationalist, and though a gossip, never mean-spirited in her tales. She seemed to take genuine interest in the town and its doings, and even the negative and distressing news was given with an awed sense of the absurd and grotesque to be found in life. She often had trouble sleeping at night, and she and a girlhood friend and neighbor, Sitter May, who had trouble sleeping, too, would get in her car and ride around until they felt drowsy.

One such night they discovered that one of their contemporaries, a friend of Aaron's, would get drunk and leave his house and at one or two in the morning, head for the courthouse and begin climbing the pecan trees on the courthouse lawn. Once they made this discovery they would drive out every night to watch him silently, drunkenly, climbing the trees. For my mother, who rarely left our house except for the occasional visits to the Garretts', Fannie Mae was the source of information about all such goings-on, and a chronicler of romances, legitimate and illegitimate too.

Part VIII

My freshman class at Wharton High School. I'm in the front row, far left.

Chapter 25

In the fall of 1931, at fifteen, I began my senior year at Wharton High School.

I was selected to be the editor of the school annual, and I knew I was to be cast in the senior play, which wouldn't begin rehearsals until the spring.

My father had hopes the Democrats would nominate Roosevelt for president at their convention the coming summer.

"He'd get us all straightened out," my father said.

"Straightened out from what?" I wanted to know.

"This depression that's going to destroy us all if something isn't done about it. The farmers are starving. You can't give cotton away. The Republicans and Wall Street have about ruined the country."

It didn't seem to me we were any worse off now than we had been ever since I could remember. My father's business was always precarious, cotton was never worth anything and the cotton farmers were almost always about to go broke, except in 1918, a time I knew about only because of what my father had told me.

"I don't know why anybody wants to be a cotton farmer in the

first place," I said. "It's always something with the cotton farmers. Either the price is too low, or the rains ruin the crops, or the
boll weevil gets it, or Johnson grass chokes it out."

"You don't know what you're talking about, Son. The farmer is
the backbone of our country and don't you forget it. For all their
troubles I tell you I envy the farmers, in my heart I envy them. I
know it's a rough life and it can be heartbreaking sometimes, but
I tell you they are fortunate in many ways. They have little overhead, and they can raise their own food, and if they're industrious
they can accumulate a little. Have some cows and some hogs and
some chickens."

"Are the banks going to go broke here?" I asked.

"What are you talking about, Son?"

"I read in the paper that banks are going broke all over the
country, that's what I'm talking about."

"Not here," my father said. "Our banks are safe, thank God. I
tell you what I heard today, though. You know it's about time for
Dude Arthur's tent show?"

"Yessir."

"He won't be coming."

"How do you know?"

"A drummer came into the store yesterday and said he ran
into him over in East Texas someplace, and Dude said they were
having to call it quits. He wasn't making it."

My mother came into the room then.

"Oh, I tell you it's serious."

"What's serious?" she wanted to know.

"This depression. People here in Wharton are worried to
death. The merchants are all complaining."

"Could you go broke?" I wanted to know.

"No. Thank God. I don't think so, as long as I can keep my overhead down to nothing."

I was suddenly struck by fear. I could see my father bankrupt. His store closed by the bank and our being evicted from our home.

"Do we own our house?" I asked.

"Yes, we do. And thank God in the State of Texas, they can never take a man's home from him. We'll always have a home."

"Papa gave you this house, didn't he?"

"He gave it to your mother."

"He gave it to you too, now, hon."

"No, he didn't, darling. I'm not sensitive and I love this house and wouldn't change a nail in it, and I'm grateful for it, but I read the note he sent you at the time and it said Hallie, your mama wants me to build you a house, and I'm going to do it."

"But when it was finished and he was making the deed out he wanted it in both our names and you refused."

"Why, Daddy?" I wanted to know.

"Because I was a poor boy and she had a rich father and I didn't want anyone to think I was marrying her for her money."

"No one thought that, hon, now you know that."

"No, I don't know that. People here can be very funny. Anyway, having it in your name was how I wanted it."

"Dad."

"Yes."

"I talked to Miss Murphree today and she said if I were going to dramatic school next fall, I'd better decide on the school now and make an application. She said she thought I should go to the

Emerson school in Boston instead of New York City, but I don't want to go to the Emerson school."

"Why?"

"Because they teach elocution and I don't want that."

"What's elocution?" he wanted to know.

"I don't know exactly, but I don't want it. I know that much."

"Well, you can't go to New York," he said, getting very excited. "I'm not going to turn a fifteen-year-old boy loose in New York."

"I'll be sixteen by the time I graduate."

"Well, that's too young to be turned loose in New York too," and he seemed very angry as he spoke.

"Mama heard from Aunt Bo in California," my mother said, "and she says there is a well-known theater school in Pasadena. She says several movie stars have been discovered doing plays there."

"What movie stars?" I wanted to know.

"Gloria Stuart and Onslow Stevens are two names I wrote down. Did you ever hear of them?" she asked.

"Yes, I've heard of them," I said, "but they are not movie stars."

"What are they, honey?" she asked.

"They're in movies. But they are what are called supporting players."

"Oh, I see. Well, anyway, they were discovered in Pasadena at the Playhouse. Did you ever hear of the Pasadena Playhouse?"

"Yes, ma'm. I've read about it."

"Where?"

"In movie magazines."

"Oh. Pasadena is a lovely town, I've always heard. Aunt Mag

and Uncle Walt live in Los Angeles and that's close by. So you would have some family near you."

"I tell you what, Son," my father said. "I've been wanting to talk to you about this. Things are a little tight for your dad right now, and it would help me a lot if you postponed going off to dramatic school for a year."

"A year, Daddy? A year?"

"You'll only be seventeen, Son."

"Could I go to New York then?"

"I don't think so, not at seventeen."

"What will I do if I don't go next year?"

"You can work in the store with me full-time."

"Yessir."

"I swear to you, Son, this is just a postponement. I'll get you off to dramatic school. I swear to you."

"Mama says Aunt Bo is sending us a brochure about the Pasadena Playhouse," my mother said.

"Yes, ma'm," I said.

My brother Tom Brooks came in then. He had his saxophone and began to practice. A car honked outside. I looked out the window and saw it was my cousin Nannie Bennett. I went out on the porch and she called from her car, "Come on with me. I have to get some groceries."

"Just a minute," I said. I went back into the house.

"Nannie is out there. She wants me to go shopping with her."

"Don't stay long," Mother said. "We'll have supper in about forty minutes."

"Yes'm," I said.

I ran out of the house and down the porch steps, down the sidewalk to Nannie's waiting car.

* * *

When I was eleven my cousin Nannie Bennett from Angleton came to Wharton to live. She had married Bolton Outlar, and had spent the first year of her marriage in New Orleans, where Bolton was serving his internship at Charity Hospital in that city. When the year was over, he and Nannie moved to Wharton and he began his medical practice. During the first year they lived with his recently widowed mother, across the street from my grandmother, who was Nannie's aunt. Nannie was full of high spirits, beautiful in her way, and a complete extrovert. She spent a great deal of time that first year visiting at my grandmother's house, and at ours, and a close bond grew up between us. I felt comfortable enough with her soon after we met to tell her of my ambitions, and though she always referred to my goal of being an actor as wanting to be a movie star, she didn't think my goal impossible or impractical. To me she seemed very theatrical and glamorous. At the University of Texas she had been elected to the beauty page, and the same year Texas A&M, then an all-male school, chose her as one of their beauties. Also, she had been to New York City several times and had seen many Broadway shows, mostly musicals. I couldn't get enough of her stories of those shows and of life in New York City, which she made to sound very glamorous. Bolton's practice as a young doctor kept him away from home all hours of the night and often she would call me to stay with her until he came back home.

I was fond of Bolton, too, and sometimes when he had a call late at night in the country, he would ask me to ride out with him and talk to him to keep him from falling asleep.

Nannie loved to dance, had in her day won Charleston contests, and at the drop of a hat would do the Charleston for you and the

Black Bottom. Early in their marriage she and Bolton came to the dances at the opera house. She was aware of all the drinking and the wife swapping, which she discussed with me openly. She let it be known to everyone, however, that while she was no prude and didn't judge others' behavior, she had married the husband she wanted and was interested in no other man. She was an only child and had been adored by her father, who had died in his early forties when she was a freshman at college. She was very close to her mother, too, but since her mother remained in Angleton in Wharton the Brooks family became her family.

My grandfather was dead by the time Nannie came to live in Wharton, and though she had known and respected him, she let me know that he wasn't above being criticized. One day when we were discussing our family, she told me that her mother felt Papa had influenced his brother Billy wrongly.

"Wrongly, in what way?" I wanted to know.

"Oh, you know that mess about Uncle Billy and his first wife, Aunt Anita," she said.

"What mess?"

"You didn't know about it?"

"No."

"Well, I'm not sure of what all happened, but for some reason Uncle Billy thought Aunt Anita was being unfaithful, and Uncle Tom thought so too, and they got guns and went after the man she was supposed to have been unfaithful with. Some of my family along with the Peter Gautier Brookses feel she was falsely accused, and wonder, too, if it had been true, why did Cousin Anita and Mabel . . ."

"Who is Mabel?" I interrupted.

"Uncle Billy and Aunt Anita's daughter," Nannie said, and

then, without breaking stride, "Why did they flee to Grandma Brooks in East Columbia for refuge, and why did Grandma Brooks take them in and let them live with her for four months? Now, please tell me why, if she was guilty of infidelity, would she ever go to Grandma Brooks in East Columbia in the first place and why would Grandma Brooks let her stay on for four months?"

"Did they kill the man?" I asked.

"What man?"

"The man she was supposedly unfaithful with."

"I don't know. I never heard about it if they did, but they probably didn't because if they had there would have been a trial, and we would certainly know about that."

"Where is Aunt Anita?"

"Living in San Antonio and married again to a very rich man and happily, too, I hear."

"How long ago did all this happen?" I wanted to know.

"Oh, Lord, let's see." Nannie paused, thinking. "Cousin Mabel is Nannie Mae Brooks's age, or maybe a little older, and Nannie Mae Brooks is about forty and Cousin Mabel was three when her mother took her to East Columbia. You mean you never heard of any of this before?"

"No," I said.

"The Peter Gautier Brookses keep in touch with them. They say Cousin Mabel has turned into a beautiful woman, and Cousin Anita is very handsome, but a little too stout, but what I can't understand is why did Uncle Billy, if he was so particular about his wife's behavior, why did he turn around and marry Aunt Ida?"

* * *

That night on our front porch I was sitting with Mother and Daddy. There was a full moon and the yard and the porch were flooded with light.

"Mother?"

"Yes, Son?"

"I didn't know Uncle Billy had two wives."

"Yes, he did. Who told you that?"

"Nannie," I said.

"Why was she telling you about Uncle Billy?" my mother asked.

"I don't know. She just got to talking about it. She told me he and Papa thought his first wife was being unfaithful, and got guns to kill the man she was supposed to be unfaithful with, and she had to flee to Grandma Brooks in East Columbia. Nannie said some members of our family thought Papa and Uncle Billy behaved unfairly, and that Grandma Brooks had taken Anita's side."

"Well, I don't know about all of that, Son."

"Do you think Papa behaved unfairly?" I asked.

"I don't know, Son. I've heard Mama say she thought he regretted getting mixed up in it. He and Uncle Billy were so different, you know. Papa was a devoted churchgoer, never drank whiskey in his life, and Uncle Billy drank to excess and never entered a church. But Papa adored him, didn't he, hon?"

"Yes, he did," my father affirmed, "and your uncle Billy was very smart."

"Papa never drank whiskey in his life?" I asked.

"Well, I won't swear that he never drank any whiskey in his

life, but he certainly didn't as long as I knew him," my mother said.

"Baboo puts whiskey in her pecan cake," I said. "And he used to eat that."

"Yes," my mother said. "But cooking changes whiskey."

"In what way?" I wanted to know.

"Well, it can't make you drunk," she said.

"Oh," I said.

"Aunt Loula called it tipsy cake," my father said, "when she made it."

"Why did she call it that if it couldn't make you drunk?" I wanted to know.

"That's just Miss Loula," my mother said. "She exaggerates everything."

"You know what else Nannie told me?" I said. "Nannie told me that Aunt Ida was supposed to have had affairs openly and everybody in town gossiped about her. Did she?"

"I don't know about that, Son," my mother said. "There was a lot of gossip, that is true."

"Nannie said she never saw her, but she had heard she was glamorous and a regular femme fatale."

"Well, she wasn't," my father said. "I can tell you that much about her. She was plain, almost severe-looking, wasn't she, hon?"

"I'd say so," my mother agreed.

"And I'll tell you this much too. She drove the wildest horses in town, could curse like a sailor and smoke and drank openly." My father laughed then, thinking of her. "She was a hellion all right. I was scared of the horses she drove, but more scared of her.

Sometimes I would be in town, when she'd drive up in her buggy, stop at one of the stores, see me and call, Boy, what's your name?"

"Horton, Miss Ida."

"Horton—what's your last name?"

"Foote, Miss Ida."

"Well, Foote, come here and hold these horses while I go in and spend some money."

"I would want to say, I'm scared to, I'm afraid of those mean horses of yours, but I was more afraid of her than the horses, so I said nothing, but took hold of their reins and prayed they wouldn't drag me through the town."

"I was scared of her too," my mother said.

"Why were you scared of her?" I wanted to know.

"She was very sarcastic. Whenever Uncle Billy would bring her over to the house, she would say very cutting things to Mama and Papa. Someone told Mama that Aunt Ida said it was so boring at our house she couldn't stand to go. All she said she'd hear was, look at little Hallie, look at little Laura, look at sweet little Rosa."

"She was a hellion," my father repeated.

"How did Uncle Billy take all of this, Mother?"

"He was humiliated, Mama always said," my mother answered, "but he just endured it, until the day he died."

"How did he die?"

"Ruptured appendix. It almost killed Papa. He was devoted to Uncle Billy. Aunt Ida came to the funeral drunk. Papa was so mortified. She kept saying over and over, What in the world am I going to do without Billy?"

"Is she still alive?"

"No, she's long since dead."

"Did you go to her funeral?"

"No."

"Did Papa and Baboo?"

"I don't remember. I'm sure they did."

Chapter 26

When I was thirteen a relative of ours was getting married in East Columbia and Nannie asked me and my girlfriend Martha Jay to go with her. We left Wharton at three in the afternoon. Jimmy Pitts, the black man that worked for her, was driving. About ten miles before East Columbia a cow ran across the road and, to avoid hitting it, Jimmy Pitts put on the brakes and the car skidded and then turned over, landing in a ditch. I was sitting in front with Jimmy Pitts and we were shaken up quite a bit but otherwise unhurt. Nannie and Martha Jay were in the backseat with the wedding presents, mostly glass. We managed to climb out of the car someway and we could see right away that Martha Jay was bleeding from cuts on her face, but Nannie looked all right. A passing car stopped and went immediately into West Columbia for help. An ambulance and relatives from East Columbia arrived soon after, and it was discovered then that Nannie was seriously hurt, broken glass having cut her severely near her kidneys. The ambulance rushed her to a Houston hospital and she was two months recuperating.

Soon after Nannie's return to Wharton from the hospital she

became pregnant, and she had a difficult pregnancy. The baby, a son named Bolton, was born prematurely, and he was sickly the first months of his life. Nannie's mother came to stay with her until the baby was declared out of danger.

I was in her house a great deal during all of this time to keep her company, as she wanted to stay with the baby as much as possible. She loved to talk about her trips to New York and I loved hearing her stories. She had saved all her theater programs and she would describe the shows to me over and over again. When she got tired of that, she would take down a scrapbook with pictures and accounts in the newspaper about her wedding. Some days she would take down the yearbooks from Texas A&M and Texas University and show me her pictures on the beauty page.

The baby, who was nicknamed Sunny, was a year old the night my father told me I should delay acting school a year. He was in the car in the backseat with his nurse, Juanita, a white girl of Czech descent, whom I had known in school, though she was older.

"How are you doing?" Nannie asked as I got into the car and then,

"Say hello to Sunny."

"Hello, Sunny."

Sunny smiled at me and I smiled back.

"Nannie," I said. "Guess what my daddy just told me?"

"What?"

"Dude Arthur has closed down his tent show."

"No. My heavens! Did you ever see the Dude Arthur tent show?" Nannie asked Juanita.

"Yes, ma'm. My sister had a few dates with Mickey Arthur when they were in Wharton last," Juanita said.

"Did she like him?" Nannie asked.

"No, she said he was very fast. She had a date with a man from a carnival and she said he was fast too."

"Mickey Arthur played the juvenile roles, Nannie," I said.

"I know that," she said. "Why did they shut down?"

"Because of the Depression."

"Oh, I am so sick of hearing about the Depression," she said. "Bolton came home last night with a long face and said we have to start economizing. Why, I said. Because of the Depression, he said. Ye gods, I'm so sick of hearing about it."

"Nannie."

"Yes."

"Daddy just told me I can't go off to school next year. He can't afford it."

"Maybe Aunt Daisy will send you."

"No, Daddy wouldn't let her."

"What will you do?" Nannie asked.

"Work at the store. He said he'd send me off next year."

"What school are you going to?" Juanita asked.

"I don't know."

"Do you want to be a lawyer?" Juanita asked.

"No. An actor."

"What kind of a school do you go to to learn something like that?" Juanita asked, sounding very puzzled.

"An acting school."

"You still want to go to New York?" Nannie asked.

"Yes, but I can't. They say I'm too young."

"What will you do when you get out of school?" Juanita asked.

"Act, I hope," I answered.

"Where?" she asked.

"Wherever I can get a job."

"In a tent show?" she wanted to know.

"No, ye gods, Juanita," Nannie said. "He doesn't want to go with a tent show."

"Maybe you'll be a movie star," Juanita said.

After supper that night I felt restless and asked permission to go and see my cousins Willa and Bertsie Horton.

"Have you studied?" Mother asked.

"No. We have no homework."

"All right, then."

It was dark when I left the house, and I took the dirt road to town through Great-Uncle Ed Hawes's cotton fields. They hadn't planted cotton there for two years, and the fields were filled with weeds. The autumn before, Dude Arthur had used one of the lots for his tent show, and I had gone several times. Mrs. Arthur, who had always played the ingenue roles, played character roles that year, wearing a white wig.

"Why has she done that?" I asked my father.

"Because she's getting old, Son. She told Dude she felt like a fool playing ingenues at her age."

"How old is she?"

"Fifty, if she's a day."

I walked through town, empty now except for the people in the drugstore having drinks or sandwiches. I went past Mr. Jack Crawford's filling station where my grandfather had his heart attack, past the vacant lot where my great-grandfather Horton's house had been, past Great-Aunt Loula's house, where she and Uncle Doc were sitting on the porch.

"Where are you going, Sonny?" she called out.

"To see Willa and Bertsie," I said.

"Have a good time," she called back.

I went on past the boardinghouse where my mother and father had taken their meals when they first married, on past the house they lived in when I was born. Up ahead I saw Willa and Bertsie's house. The lights were on in almost every room.

Willa, Bertsie and Mabel, the second sister, who had married my uncle Brother, had had a difficult life. Their mother, Mabel, died at forty-two during the flu epidemic of 1918, of a broken heart my mother and father always insisted, although the cause of death was officially listed as the flu. She was not a Wharton native and how and where she met her husband, my great-uncle Albert, I've never known. However, at the time of their marriage Albert was a prosperous merchant, "the best merchant I have ever known," my father always claimed. He built a house for his young bride soon after their marriage, and his sisters warmly welcomed her into the family, secretly hoping that she would influence him to give up his obsessive habit of gambling.

She wasn't able to, and sometimes, my mother said, he would stay out all night, and these nights, she would send Willa, the oldest daughter, to go to the house where the games were held to see if she could find him. When their mother died, Willa was sixteen, Mabel thirteen and Bertsie, named Alberta Louisiana Texas Patience, for her father and Great-Aunt Loula, eight.

Their father in the meantime had lost his store because of gambling debts, and was clerking for Mr. Dave Dickson. He and his sisters decided that he would rent his house out and send one daughter to each of his sisters. Willa went to live with Loula, Mabel with Reenie and Bertsie with Lida. Reenie died in 1927, the year Mabel graduated from high school. Willa at eighteen was the first to marry and went to live with her husband in San Antonio, but she divorced him after a few years and came back to Wharton, living again for a while with her aunt Loula. Mabel was married by then to my uncle Brother, and Bertsie was a secretary at the gas company.

Soon Willa and Bertsie decided to move back to their family home. Their father moved into the house with them for a while, and I suppose supported them, but after a year, he moved out again and began living openly with a woman accused of being a prostitute. He now owned and operated a pool hall, and he and his woman friend lived over it.

When I reached my cousins' house I went in without knocking. Hearing voices in the back, I went toward the kitchen, calling, "Bertsie. Willa."

"Come on back, Little Horton, we're in the kitchen," Willa answered. They were there with Celleste, the black cook who had worked for my great-aunt Lida ever since I could remember.

"Well, lookie here, Little Horton is grown into a man," Celleste greeted me.

"Where have you been keeping yourself, Celleste?"

"I've retired, sugar, except when Mrs. Abell has company and wants me to cook the company dinner."

"Celleste has come over to get Bertsie to talk to her mama. Her mama was given some Christmas checks and she still won't let Celleste cash them for her," Willa said.

"My mama, I hate to say, is teched," Celleste said. "Old age has got her. She's hid those checks somewhere in the house and I can't find them. She thinks Bertsie hung the moon and if anybody can get them from her, she can."

"I'll try, honey," Bertsie said.

Bertsie had a stack of movie star pictures before her on the table. As a young girl she had wanted to get into the movies, and was an avid collector of movie star pictures and knew all about their lives, or at least what movie magazines said were their lives.

"Why do you have your movie star pictures out, Bertsie?" I wanted to know.

"I've outgrown them, honey," Bertsie said.

"About time," Willa said, giggling.

"Susan Dela Fields's daughter is sending for them now. She wants to be a movie star, her mama says, so I'm giving them to her."

"I thought you wanted to be a movie star, Bertsie," Celleste said.

"How am I going to get to be a movie star in Wharton, Texas?" Bertsie said.

"Well, don't stay in Wharton, Texas," Willa said. "Go on out to Hollywood."

"On what?" Bertsie said.

"Ask your daddy to send you," I said.

"Fat chance," Bertsie said.

"Are you going to Hollywood to study acting?" Willa wanted to know.

"I don't know where I'm going," I said. "I want to go to New York, but I can't do that, my daddy said."

"Why?" Willa asked.

"Because he says I'm too young. Anyway, I can't go anywhere until next year. My daddy hasn't got the money to send me."

"It's the Depression," Willa said.

"What's the Depression?" Bertsie wanted to know.

"Come on, Bebe," Willa said. (She often called Bertsie Bebe, because she said she reminded her of the actress Bebe Daniels.) "Nobody has any money, because of the Depression."

"Roosevelt is going to fix all that," Bertsie said, "if he gets nominated and elected."

"You remember Virginia Neff?" Willa asked me. "We graduated together and she went off to New Orleans and then on to New York, where she was working. Lived there for five years, but she lost her job last month and she's back home now. She is coming over tonight."

"What did she do in New York?"

"I don't know. I never asked her."

When my great-aunt Reenie died in 1927, Great-Aunt Lida and Bertsie moved over to her house to make a home for her husband, Uncle Alec, who was terribly grieved by Aunt Reenie's death. Celleste went with them. Uncle Alec became more and more despondent and one day committed suicide. It was Celleste who found his body and her screams when she discovered he was dead could be heard all over that part of town. Ever after that she claimed she saw his ghost walking about the house.

"Did you ever see him after he died, Bertsie?" I asked.

"No, thank God," Bertsie said.

"Mabel saw the lady in white at Aunt Loula's," Willa said. "It almost scared her to death."

"Hush up talking about all that," Bertsie said.

"Well, I saw Mr. Alec just as plain as I'm seeing you right now. I saw him once in the kitchen, and once in the living room and twice in the bedroom," Celleste said.

"Did he speak to you?" I wanted to know.

"No, dear God," Celleste said.

"Did you speak to him?" Willa asked.

"No, ma'm. You know better than that. Mama says she saw him once in our house, and I said, Mama, you're just making that up. He don't even know where we live. He do, too, she said, and he asked me plain as day is Celleste home? I said, Mama, you ought to be ashamed of yourself telling lies like that."

"Is that the only ghost you've seen?" Willa asked.

"Yes, ma'm," she said, "and all I care to see."

"I expect so," Willa said.

"I've got to go on back to Mama's," Celleste said, "before Mama sets the house on fire. She's always lighting matches to light the gas stove, without first turning on the gas."

"I'll be over tomorrow to talk to your mama," Bertsie said.

"Yes, ma'm. Thank you," Celleste said as she left the room. I began to look through Bertsie's movie star pictures.

"Who is your favorite movie star?" I asked.

"Oh, I don't know. Barbara La Marr was the most beautiful."

"Barbara La Marr? I never heard of her."

"She was before your time," Bertsie said.

"She's been dead a long time," Willa said.

"Oh, a long time," Bertsie added. "She was too beautiful to live, they said."

"Who said?" I wanted to know.

"I don't know," Bertsie said. "I read that someplace."

Bertsie began to look through the photographs and found one of Barbara La Marr. She handed it to me.

"She was pretty," I said.

"Beautiful," Bertsie echoed. "Too beautiful to live. See what it says? To Bertsie, Lest Ye Forget, Barbara La Marr."

"Willa," a woman's voice called from the hallway.

"Come on back, Ginger, we're in the kitchen," Willa called back.

Bertsie took Barbara La Marr's picture from me and put it back with the others.

Virginia Neff came into the room then and Willa went over to her and they kissed each other.

"Ginger," Willa said, "this is my cousin Horton."

"Heh," Virginia said.

She had very fair skin, lightly freckled, and dyed red hair. She was simply but stylishly dressed.

"I hear you lived in New York," I said.

"Yes."

"I hope to go to New York one day."

"He wants to be an actor," Willa said.

"Oh, well," Virginia said. "That's the place to go."

"Did you know many actors in New York?" I asked.

"A few," she said. "None you would ever have heard of probably."

"Punkin Armstrong's husband was a walk-on in a play at the Theatre Guild," Bertsie said.

"What play?" I asked.

"*Liliom,*" Willa said.

"I saw that," Virginia said.

"Then you saw Punkin Armstrong's husband," Willa said.

"If I did, I didn't know it," Virginia said.

"They've divorced now," Willa said. "She's back here too. It's the Depression. Everyone is coming back."

"Where did you live in New York?" I asked.

"The Village. New York is expensive. Even the Village is expensive now."

"Is that Greenwich Village?" I asked.

"Yes," Virginia said.

"Artists live there," I said.

"Yes, they do," Virginia said.

"Actors, too?" I asked.

"Yes," Virginia said.

"My cousin Nannie," I said, "has been to New York and seen lots of shows, and she saw a musical with Ruby Keeler."

"What was the name of it?" Willa asked.

"I forgot the name of it," I said, "but anyway she was married to Al Jolson at the time, and the afternoon Nannie saw the show, he was in the audience, and when Ruby Keeler came out to tap-dance to a song, I think called 'Liza,' he stood up spontaneously in the audience and began to sing while she danced. She said the audience went crazy."

"Do you think it was spontaneous?" Willa asked.

"I don't know," I said. "I guess so."

"I don't," Willa said. "I'll bet my life it was planned."

"Maybe," I said.

"Well, we'll never see Al Jolson and Ruby Keeler in this town. All we get is Dude Arthur," Bertsie said.

"You won't anymore," I said. "He's quit because of the Depression."

I wanted to keep on talking about New York, but Virginia seemed more interested in asking Willa about their friends from high school. Soon it was nine o'clock and I knew my parents would expect me home since it was a school night, so I said good-bye.

When I again passed my great-aunt Loula's house, she and Uncle Doc were still on the porch, and she called out to me as I walked by.

"How were the girls?"

"Fine," I said.

"You'll soon be graduating, Sonny."

"Yes, ma'm," I said.

"I'm going to give you a dance for your graduation," she said.

"Thank you, ma'm," I said.

"Good night, Sonny," she said.

"Good night," I said, and continued on home.

Part IX

*Taken when I was fourteen in the backyard
of my father's rent house, a house he sold in
order to send me to drama school.*

Chapter 27

It was after the Christmas holidays that I began to realize that I really was about to graduate from school. Everyone in our class, there were twenty-eight of us, was talking constantly now about being seniors and what it meant to be seniors and what we were going to do when we graduated. At least half of the girls, including Martha Jay, were planning to go to college, but most of them were talking of going to state schools because those were cheaper and it was a depression and their families had no money. Most of the boys didn't even think of going to college and were already looking for jobs.

It was a busy time for me. Being editor of the school annual took much more time than I had imagined, and I still went to the store every day after school to work for my father. He was very understanding, though, when my annual duties kept me after school.

Two weeks before play rehearsals were to begin Miss Murphree (I still called her Miss Murphree even though she was only six years older than I) asked me to read the play she had selected as our senior play. It was called *Not So Long Ago,* and had been done on Broadway, she told me. She asked me to get back to her as soon as I'd read it, as she had something of importance to discuss with me. I immediately tried to imagine what she wanted to discuss. I began reading the play as soon as I got to my father's store and finished before supper. I don't remember much about the play now except it was set in the nineteenth century, and none of it seemed very relevant to me.

The next day after school I went to Miss Murphree's room and told her I had read the play.

"How did you like it?" she said.

"It's OK."

"You don't seem very enthusiastic," she said.

"No, I like it," I said, lying because I didn't like it at all, really.

"It was done in New York a while back, nineteen twenty-five, I believe. It was one of the first parts Eva Le Gallienne played."

"Who's that?" I asked.

"You want to be an actor and you've never heard of Eva Le Gallienne?"

"I'm sorry. No, I haven't."

"She's the head of the Civic Repertory Theatre in New York City and a great actress."

"What's that?"

"What's what?"

"The kind of theater you said she was head of."

"The Civic Repertory Theatre. It's a famous theater in New York, where they do classic plays in repertory."

"What's repertory?"

"Where they do a different play every night."

"Oh. I guess I must sound awful ignorant to you," I said.

"Forgive me, Horton," she said. "I don't mean to be condescending; when I was your age I wouldn't have known about Eva Le Gallienne either."

"Yes, ma'm," I said.

"Now," she said. "I want to talk to you about casting the play."

"Yes, ma'm," I said.

"You know," she said, "in a play, often the most interesting parts are not the leads, the straight parts, so to speak, but the character parts."

"Why?"

"Because you don't just play yourself," she said.

"Yes, ma'm," I said.

"Now you know usually I cast you in the lead," she said.

"Yes, ma'm," I said.

"But this time unless you object I would like to cast you in the character part."

My heart sank. I didn't want to play a character part.

"I think you'll have a lot of fun doing it, and the audience will love you. What do you think?"

I didn't answer right away, and then decided I'd better be truthful.

"I don't want to play that part," I said.

"Oh?"

"I want to play the lead."

"But that part is so dull."

"But that's what I want to play."

"All right, if that's what you want to do."

There was silence then. I knew she was upset with me, and I was sorry.

"I hear you won't go off to acting school next year. Will you stay on here?"

"No, ma'm. My grandmother is going to Dallas for the year. Billy is going to a night law school there and she wants to be with him. Last night my father said if I will get a job I can go with her and study acting in Dallas."

"Are there any places to study in Dallas?"

"Yes. As soon as my father said I could go to Dallas, I called my aunt Laura who lives there and she looked in the phone book and found there was an acting school called Mrs. Woodward's School of Dramatic Art. So I'll study there next year if I like the school, then the next year my daddy says he will have the money to send me away to acting school out of state."

"Have you decided where you want to go?"

"Pasadena Playhouse. My aunt Bo, my grandmother's sister, sent me a catalog about it. Pasadena is near Hollywood and Los Angeles."

"What about the school I told you about?"

"The Emerson school?"

"Yes, in Boston, the one I told you my instructor in college had gone to for a summer course. She liked it a lot."

"My folks want me to go to Pasadena. I have two great-aunts and some cousins out there."

"Would you bring me the catalog so I can see it?"

"Of the Pasadena Playhouse?"

"Yes. I'd just like to take a look at it."

"Sure."

"Rehearsals will begin next week."

"Yes, ma'm."

"We may have to rehearse at night. You seniors have so much

to do getting ready for graduation. I swear none of you are paying much attention to your classes. I hope you'll take the play rehearsals seriously. I always count on you."

"Yes, ma'm. Thank you."

It was an increasingly busy time as graduation day got closer. There were invitations to the graduation ceremonies to be ordered and sent and presents had already begun to arrive from relatives and friends. Everyone in town knew I liked to read so I was given a great number of books, though unfortunately not many that I wanted: *Letters from a Merchant to His Son, Sketches of Famous Americans, A Guide to the Holy Land,* five copies of *David Copperfield* (I already had two) and *The Raven,* a biography of Sam Houston, which I also already had a copy of, given to me in my junior year by the DAR for writing the best essay on Sam Houston. My great-aunt Loula, when she heard what I had won, said she bet Governor Horton was turning over in his grave, as he despised Sam Houston, and she herself thought he was a common old reprobate. There were also other books, whose titles I've forgotten, besides shirts, ties, handkerchiefs and checks (including one for a hundred dollars from my grandmother, a fortune to me).

Then there was a series of dinner parties and dances given in my honor by relatives and friends. My mother and father gave me the first dinner party at our house, and everyone in the senior class was invited. Great-Aunt Loula gave the dance she promised at her house, and again invited my whole class, and Nannie gave a smaller dinner party at her house. Then there were picture show parties, and dinners hosted by friends and relatives at the Plaza Hotel, always including my brothers and my mother and father, and always featuring a present at my place at the table. Soon the presents were so numerous that my mother had to put up three bridge tables in our living room to display all the gifts. My mother insisted I write everyone a thank-you note right away and I complained bitterly, but I finally gave in and got it done.

All my relatives came by to look at my presents and said they had never seen so many before, and my mother said she hadn't either, and was just overcome by the generosity of my family and friends.

Finally graduation day arrived. Frances Campbell and Lucy Forgason were valedictorian and salutatorian. I had the highest average of any of the boys. My mother said I could have been valedictorian or at least salutatorian if I had applied myself, but my father said, "I think Son has done very well. I wouldn't want him to become an educated fool with no common sense like some I know."

Chapter 28

The early summer of 1932 I worked again at my father's store, but I had my nights free with no schoolwork to worry about. I went to dances with Martha Jay at the opera house until the weather was so hot it made dancing unbearable, I went to the picture show, although I don't remember a single film, and I read a great deal. I went into Houston often on Sundays with my grandmother and my uncles Speed and Billy. My grandmother would visit with her sisters and we would go to the movies. Houston had three first-run movie houses then, the Metropolitan, the Kirby and the Majestic.

I remember once when I was eleven, my father, feeling I suppose that being in the store such long hours six days a week left him little time to spend with me, asked me if the next Sunday I would like to go to Houston with him, just the two of us, and said that we would do only what I wanted. I said I would and that what I'd like would be to go to all three picture shows. And that's what we did. We got up at four in the morning to catch the five o'clock train to Houston. We arrived in Houston at seven-thirty, had breakfast and went to the morning show at the Kirby, had dinner, went to the Metropolitan in the afternoon, had supper and went to the Majestic that night, getting out at nine o'clock and catching the night train back to Wharton.

Riding back to the train station, I thought of the last time I had been to Houston, with my father, my mother and my grandmother who wanted to see *The Singing Fool* with Al Jolson, which was playing at the Metropolitan. We were warned that it was sad, and since my father's favorite actors were Charlie Chaplin, Harry Langdon and Buster Keaton, I wondered how he was going to take *The Singing Fool*. The audience was very quiet and very attentive as the film unfolded, when all of a sudden I became aware of someone sobbing. I thought it was my mother or my grandmother, but when I looked around, I learned to my surprise that it was my father, sobbing uncontrollably. Riding home that evening he said, "In my opinion there ought to be a law against making pictures that sad."

Three weeks after graduation, my grandmother told me we would leave for Dallas in August, so she could get settled in her rented house. I had never spent more than a day away from Wharton except for the three summers I visited with my grandmother Cleveland in Houston for a week, had never worked for anyone but my father, had never taken a streetcar by myself, and of course I had never been to a dramatic school of any kind.

My grandmother found a comfortable house not far from my aunt Laura in Oak Cliff, a suburb of Dallas, and the first thing she did was hire a cook. Billy registered again for night classes at his law school, and Speed began looking for work.

My grandmother took me to see Miss Woodrow at the Woodward School. I liked her at once, and my grandmother arranged for me to start classes the next week. What did I learn? What was I taught? I can tell you exactly what I was taught at the Pasadena Playhouse and later on by Tamara Daykarhonova, Vera Soloviova and Andrius Jilinsky at Daykarhonova's school in New York City, but what Miss Woodrow taught me or tried to teach me I can't remember at all. I remember that she said there would be a recital in the spring and each of the students would perform. I was assigned *Swan Song*, a one-act play by Chekhov. I had never heard of Chekhov. The play had only two characters, one of them an aging actor who wakes up hungover backstage in a theater, where he feels he has just given a brilliant performance. But his fellow performers have all gone off and left him alone and drunk, and he is bitter. The theater's prompter is there, however, and comes in to befriend him, and as the play unfolds the old actor does speeches from *King Lear, Hamlet* and *Othello.* Now why Miss Woodrow chose *Swan Song* for a sixteen-year-old boy to perform, I can't imagine, but at the time I didn't doubt for a moment that I could act it and act it very well. I do remember this about Miss Woodrow, she gave me a feeling of great confidence in my ability, and whatever her method was I thank her for that.

I found a job, too, as I had promised my father, ushering at the Majestic, a movie theater that had stage shows between films. Of all the films I saw, *The Animal Kingdom* with Leslie Howard and Ann Harding is the only one I remember at all, because of one line I have never forgotten, spoken by Leslie Howard: "Who but you, Daisy, who but you and strangers are honest with me ever?"

I soon learned to use the streetcar, and often took it to my work at the Majestic.

My grandmother was providing me with room and board just like she was doing for my uncles. She was also giving them an allowance every week and offered to do the same for me. Since I was making three dollars a week ushering, I declined her offer, even though after paying carfare, buying cigarettes and a few Cokes and a sandwich at the drugstore every now and then, I didn't have much left at the end of a week. One afternoon, the day before I was to get paid at the theater, I had only twenty-five cents left out of my three dollars, and on this day after work, on my way to the streetcar, I decided to stop in a drugstore for a Coke. I reached in my pocket to feel the twenty-five cents to be sure it was still there. It was, but then I decided to take it out and look at it to be sure it was twenty-five cents and not a nickel. Satisfied it was a twenty-five-cent piece I put it back in my pocket and went into the drugstore, sat down at the counter and ordered a Coke. I drank the Coke, and the counterman gave me my check (for a nickel), and when I reached in my pocket for the quarter it wasn't there. I thought, of course, I had reached into the wrong pocket and I quickly reached into the other pocket, but still no quarter. I began to perspire and I pretended that I wanted the ice in the Coke glass and slowly began chewing the ice as I wondered what to do. I felt sure the counterman would never believe my story of a lost quarter and would think I was a deadbeat and have me arrested. I cursed myself for stopping for a Coke, and then I realized that I not only couldn't pay for my Coke, but I didn't have fare for the streetcar home either. Finally I felt I had to confess my predicament to the counterman.

"Mister," I called almost inaudibly.

He was at the other end of the counter and didn't hear me. I waited a few agonizing minutes and tried again. "Mister," I said again in almost a whisper.

He started back toward me and I wasn't sure whether he had

heard me or not. I could feel my face flushing. I knew I must look so guilty that he'd think anything I said was a lie, but if he stopped and faced me, I knew I had to try and get the words out. He did stop and I must have looked terrible, because he said, "Are you feeling all right, boy?"

"Yessir."

"You look terrible. Is there something wrong?"

"Yessir."

"What is it, boy?"

"I lost my money."

"What? Speak a little louder."

"I lost my money. I had a quarter when I came in here, but I lost it, and I can't pay for my Coke."

"Oh."

"But I come by here every day and I swear to you, mister, I'll bring the nickel to you tomorrow when I come by."

"All right. Don't worry about it. I trust you," he said as he started away.

"Mister," I called, trying to catch him before he got away.

"Yes?"

"May I use the telephone so I can call my aunt to come get me? I don't have carfare now to get home either."

"All right. There's the phone there."

I went to the phone and then the horrible thought came to me, what if Aunt Laura wasn't home? I knew my grandmother and my uncles had gone to visit friends for the afternoon and they wouldn't be home. Praying, I dialed the phone and held my breath until I heard Aunt Laura's voice saying, "Hello."

"Aunt Laura."

"Yes."

"This is Horton."

"Horton, are you all right?"

"Yes, but I'm in a terrible predicament."

"What in the world is wrong, honey?"

"I went to get a Coke and I lost my quarter and now I don't have carfare to get home."

"Where are you, Son?"

I didn't know the address, so again I called to the counterman.

"Mister."

"Yes."

"Where am I?"

"What?"

"Where am I, sir?"

"You're in Dallas."

"I know that, sir, but I don't know the address of the drugstore."

He told me the address and I told it to Aunt Laura.

"I'll be right there, honey," she said, and I hung up the phone.

I wanted to ask if I could sit on a drugstore stool while I waited, but I was afraid to, so I went out to the sidewalk. It was blazing hot and there was no awning to shield me from the sun. I decided to take a chance and go back into the drugstore away from the heat. I went in as unobtrusively as possible. I had been standing the better part of the day at the theater and my feet hurt, so I decided to sneak over to one of the counter stools and sit down, trying to think of what I would say if the soda jerk asked me why I was still there. He came toward me as I sat down and I thought he was going to ask me to leave, but instead he said,

"Can I help you?" and what came into my mind was to say to

him, "*May* I help you, you certainly *can* since you are able," but instead I said, "How long will it take to get to Dallas from Oak Cliff?"

"Depends on the traffic. This time of day, God knows. Hour, forty-five minutes. You waiting for your aunt?"

"Yessir."

"Well, wait in here. It's too hot out on the sidewalk."

"Yessir. Thank you."

"You want a glass of ice water?"

"No, sir. Thank you."

Aunt Laura was there in forty-five minutes, and I was never so glad to see anyone in my life.

"What on earth," she said as I opened the door to the car.

"Do you have a nickel, Auntie?"

"Yes, I do," she said.

Opening her purse and finding a nickel she handed it to me.

"I'll be right back," I said, and went back into the drugstore.

"Here you are, mister," I said.

"OK," he said, opening the cash register and putting the nickel inside.

That night in my room when I was taking my trousers off the quarter rolled out of one of the cuffs of my pants.

That spring Mother decided to come to Dallas to see me in *Swan Song*. It was quite an event for her to get away from Wharton. She and my father had not spent a night apart since they had been married. Aunt Rosa and her baby were now living with us and she, my uncles, my aunt Laura, my grandmother and my mother all came to see me play this aging Russian actor. I can't imagine what it was like, but I remember at the time thinking it went very well, and Miss Woodrow thought so, and my family all made a great deal over me. When we got home from the school that night my father called to say Tom Brooks had fallen out of a tree and broken his collarbone and my mother would have to come home right away. She had planned to spend the weekend, but she took the bus back to Houston early the next morning.

I recently reread *Swan Song.* Chekhov describes the character I played at sixteen as a comic actor, sixty-eight years of age, who feels his talent has been wasted in comic parts. To prove to himself that he can still be superb in the great classical roles, he acts out scenes from *Hamlet* and *King Lear* for the prompter in the theater. What in the world, at sixteen, did I make of all this?

A month later we all went back to Wharton. I would be leaving soon for Pasadena, and Billy had graduated from his Dallas law school.

My grandmother gave him an office in one of her buildings and bought him the law books he would need to set himself up in practice. It took two weeks to get the office furnished with a desk, office chairs, a typewriter and bookshelves for the law books. Two days before he was to begin, a sign was painted on the office window, reading "William Brooks, Attorney-at-Law."

"Wouldn't it be wonderful if he were to settle down and have a real law practice. Mama would be so happy," my mother said to my father, sitting on our porch the night before he was to start his practice. My grandmother came over then.

"Do you mind a visitor?" she asked.

"No," my father said, "you are always welcome, Baboo, you know that."

He got up then and said, "Sit in my chair, I'll get another one."

"I'll get it," I said.

I went into the house and brought out a small rocker.

"Let me have the small chair," my grandmother said.

"No, you stay where you are," my father insisted.

"No, I really prefer the small rocker."

"All right," my father said, and my grandmother got out of her chair and sat in the rocker.

"Big Horton," she said, "I want to ask a favor of you."

"Yes, ma'm."

"I may be doing some traveling next year, and it would make me feel much easier when I'm gone if I knew the farms were being looked out for properly. Would you consider overseeing them for me?"

"Yes, ma'm, if you trust me," he said.

"You're the only person here I do trust," my grandmother said. "Of course I'll want to pay you."

"No, ma'm," he said, "I don't want anything."

"Well, I can't accept your help," she said, "if you don't let me pay you something for helping me."

"Well, we'll talk about it."

Billy came up on the porch then.

"Mama?"

"Yes, Son."

"Can I have the keys to the car?"

"Why?"

"I just want to go for a ride."

"All right. They're in my purse on my dresser. But don't stay out late. You'll want to get an early start at your office tomorrow."

"Suppose I don't have any clients?"

"Well, you may not the first day. I spoke to Junior yesterday and he said it took a while to build up a practice. You have to be patient."

"I guess."

Everybody was silent for a moment.

I looked out in the yard. Fireflies were everywhere. I thought of when I was younger and I'd catch fireflies and put them in a mason jar.

"I'll see you in the morning," Billy said, and left.

Again there was silence except for the creak of the rocking chairs.

"Well," my grandmother said, "I hope it works out for him. I know he's worried about getting clients, there are so many lawyers here and Rome wasn't built in a day."

"How many lawyers are there?" I asked.

"Let's see," my father said. "Mr. Ingram, Cousin Junior Hawes, Mr. Kelly, Steven Munson."

"We're kin to him," Mother said.

"How are we kin?" I wanted to know.

"I forgot. How are we kin, Mama?"

"It's on your papa's side of the family. Second cousins, I think."

"And we're kin to Cousin Junior Hawes," I said.

"I'm not," Mother said. "You and your daddy are."

"How are we kin to him, Daddy?" I asked.

"He's my first cousin once removed," he said.

"Is that how it is?" Mother said.

"Mr. Davis," Daddy continued, "Mr. Reed."

"That's enough," I said.

"Mr. Cline," my father continued.

"He was your uncle Billy's partner when he was alive," my grandmother said. "Your uncle Billy was a brilliant lawyer, I hope Billy will be half the lawyer he was."

Billy was in his office promptly at nine the next morning. I went with my mother and grandmother and brothers in the afternoon to see how he was getting on. He was sitting at his desk when we came in.

"Where are my clients?" he said.

"Now, Billy, you must be patient. Rome wasn't built in a day," my grandmother said.

"Maybe I'll go out to California with you, Little Horton, and start acting."

"Come along," I said.

"Look at this," Billy said, handing my grandmother a telegram.

"Who's it from?" she asked.

"Aunt Em," he said.

Aunt Em was one of my grandmother's sisters in Houston. My grandmother read the telegram.

"Read what it says, Mama," my mother asked.

"We need a lawyer in this family. Good luck and good wishes. Love, Aunt Em."

"Em's always so thoughtful," she added, after reading it.

"Did you get any other telegrams?" my brother Tom Brooks asked.

"No," Billy said. "But several people came by to wish me good luck."

"Who did?" Tom Brooks asked.

"Junior Hawes, Carl Shannon, Thomas Abell. Miss Lily Outlar, Miss Mabel."

"That was thoughtful," my grandmother said.

"It certainly was," Mother said.

"And Big Horton," Billy said, looking at his watch.

"Would somebody go to the drugstore and get me a Coke? I'm dying of thirst."

"You go," my grandmother said. "We'll stay here and if anyone comes, Little Horton can fetch you."

"All right, I'll be back in a few minutes."

The next day he was back in his office again at nine, but again there were no clients. That night he got drunk and in the morning told his mother he wasn't going back to the office ever again, and he didn't.

The night before I was to leave for California, my father called me out on the porch and said he wanted me to know he was proud of me, and he knew I would work hard and take advantage of this opportunity. My mother joined us and she said she had packed my suitcase for me and to be sure and write home once a week. I promised. My father said that he had purchased my bus ticket to Los Angeles and that my grandmother was having Billy drive me and Mother to the Houston bus station. He said he wished he could go to see me off, too, but knew I understood that he couldn't leave the store, and I said I did.

My mother said that Daddy had bought me a billfold from his store and that they had put all the money I would need for the trip inside it.

"And be careful with that wallet, Son," my father continued, "there are pickpockets on those buses, and . . ."

"Daddy, I'm going to be careful. Don't worry."

"I'm not worrying. I have every confidence in you. I'm very proud of you, Son. I know you'll do just fine."

"And Laura will meet the bus in Dallas and take you out to her house for the night and take you to the bus in the morning," my mother said.

"You'll get to see mountains. Do you realize that? I envy you," my father said. "I've never seen a mountain in my life, I guess now I never will. Mississippi and Louisiana are as flat as Texas."

"Tom Brooks is going to take over your room when you go," my mother said. "He's all excited about it. Aunt Mag and Uncle Walt will meet you at the Los Angeles bus station and I'm sure they'll take you to their house for the night and the next day take you out to the YMCA in Pasadena. The school suggested you stay there until you get registered and they assign you to a boardinghouse. Can you think of anything else to tell him, hon?"

"No, just that he should use his head, which I know he will, he always does."

"I want to go and tell Bertsie and Willa good-bye and then Nannie and Bolton."

"All right, Son. Don't stay out late. You'll have to be up early in the morning to get to Houston in time for your bus," Mother said.

"I won't stay out late. Not that I'll sleep. I'm all keyed up."

My father laughed.

"You're journey proud, that's what's wrong with you," he said.

"Well, I'm glad you're going, Son. Sometimes I wish your mother and I could get up and go and live some other place."

"Yessir. I'll see you later."

On my way to Bertsie and Willa's I thought of what my father had said about living somewhere else. I couldn't understand it, because he always seemed so content here.

As I walked through town, empty now except for the drugstore customers, it came to me that this was the last time I would be doing this until I returned next summer, and for the first time I had a feeling of sadness, of regret about going, but I deliberately turned away from those feelings, just as in recent days I had turned away from a voice that once in a while spoke to me, from where I didn't know, saying over and over, What if you have no talent? How can you make a living as an actor? What if you're not able to?

As I walked past the brick buildings my grandmother owned I saw the one that my uncle Speed had used for his cleaning and pressing shop, and the one that Billy had used for his law office, empty now, the sign "William Brooks, Attorney-at-Law" still on the window, and I wondered why things had turned out the way they did. He rode by me then in my grandmother's car. When he saw me he stopped and asked if I wanted a ride, and I thanked him, but said I would walk. I could tell he was sober and I was glad for that.

As I went by my great-aunt Loula's house I saw her and Uncle Doc again on their porch.

"Hello, Sonny," she called.

"Hello, Auntie. Hello, Uncle Doc."

"Hello, Son."

"Come here and kiss me good-bye," she said.

"Yes, ma'm."

I went up on the porch and kissed her and shook hands with Uncle Doc. He reached in his pocket and took out a silver dollar.

"Treat yourself to something in California."

"Thank you, Uncle Doc."

My aunt kissed me again.

"We are awful proud of you, Sonny."

"Thank you, Auntie."

Willa and Bertsie weren't home when I got there. I waited out in the yard for a few minutes, hoping they would come back, when Mrs. Stewart, the neighbor next door, called out to me that they had gone to the picture show. I thanked her and left.

I decided then to go look one last time at the river. I didn't want to go by my great-aunt Loula's house again, in case Aunt Loula and Uncle Doc were still on the porch, because I felt sure they would think I was crazy wanting to look at the river this time of night, so I went to the street behind their house. As I passed the house where my daddy had once told me he was born and raised until his mother and daddy separated, I paused for a minute to look at it, a small Victorian house that the Carson family lived in now. I could see one of the Carson boys walking past a window, and I wondered if he was the one that accidentally shot Milton Rush down at the River Bottoms, and I wondered what it would feel like to accidentally shoot someone, and I wondered who was the one who told Mrs. Rush her boy had been shot and killed, like my grandmother had to tell Mrs. Gifford when Mr. Hood shot Mr. Gifford. I walked on then, because I didn't want the Carsons to think I was spying on them. The river was only half a block away and when I got there I stayed at the top of the riverbank, because it was quite a climb down to the river itself. It looked so calm and peaceful in the moonlight and I thought of all the people through the years drowned in its waters. I was sorry I still couldn't swim, and I remembered that when I had complained about that last week to my parents, my daddy had said, "Maybe you'll join the YMCA in Pasadena and you can learn to swim there." I tried to imagine then what life in Pasadena was going to be like, when I heard a train coming over the train bridge, and I decided to move on. Going to Nannie's house I passed the house Leslie Crockett had lived in before his mother had left his father, and I thought about him and wondered what had become of him and would I recognize him after all these years if I passed him on the street. I went past the Nation Hotel then and my aunt Reenie's house. I thought of what my mother always said about Aunt Reenie being the amiable one in the Horton family, the peacemaker, and I thought of her death, and how grieved her husband, Uncle Alec, had been, and how everybody had said when he committed suicide that no one blamed him, because her dying had left him so grief-stricken he couldn't bear living any longer.

When I got to Nannie's house she was putting her baby to bed.

"Bolton on a call?"

"As usual," she said. "What time do you leave tomorrow?"

"Eight o'clock."

"Who's driving you?"

"Billy."

"If he's sober. Bolton said he saw him again last night drunk as a lord. Poor Aunt Daisy. How does she take it? Her boys all drunks. Uncle Tom was such a fine man. Don't you start drinking now. All these movie stars drink, you know. I have to mail a letter. You want to ride with me to the post office?"

"No, I thank you. I'd better get on home."

"Well, kiss me good-bye. Behave yourself now."

"I'll try."

I took a last look at Sunny asleep in his crib and left.

Outside on Richmond Road a cotton truck came roaring by. I waited for it to pass before crossing the street. Up ahead was my grandmother's house and I started through her yard as I'd done a million times, when I saw her sitting on her porch with my uncle Speed.

"Hi," I called out.

"Hi, Hoss," Speed said. "Come say good-bye to me."

"Won't I see you in the morning before I leave?"

"I don't think so, I have to see about a job."

I went up the porch and held out my hand.

"Well, so long then."

"Take care of yourself, Hoss."

"I'll try."

"Tell 'em out in Hollywood if they need a good-lookin' fella I'm available."

"I will."

"Good night, you-all," I said, as I started away.

"Good night, Son," my grandmother said. "I'll see you in the morning."

I realized after she spoke that she had been crying. I left them with a great feeling of sadness.

I continued on through the yard to my house. The lights were all out and so I knew my brothers were in bed. I went around the side of the house to the front. My mother and father were still on the porch.

"Is that you, Son?" my mother called out.

"Yes, ma'm."

"Come on up and sit with us for a while," Daddy said. "You'll be in Dallas this time tomorrow night."

"Yessir. I realize that."

"Are you going to miss us, Son?" Mother said.

"Sure I will. I saw Baboo just now. She and Speed were sitting on the porch. She had been crying."

"How do you know?" my mother asked.

"I could tell the way she was talking. Nannie said Bolton saw Billy uptown drunk last night."

"I know. Mama told me he came home drunk."

"What's he going to do, Mama? Will he never go back to his law practice?"

"He says he won't. He told Mama he never wanted to be a lawyer in the first place, but everybody pushed him into it because he had been named for Uncle Billy."

"As I was going to Bertsie and Willa's he came by in Baboo's car and he asked if I wanted a ride. He wasn't drinking. I could tell that," I said.

"Thank God for that," Mother said. "How were Bertsie and Willa?"

"They weren't home. Mrs. Stewart said they'd gone to the picture show. I saw Aunt Loula and Uncle Doc sitting on their porch and I said good-bye to them," I said. "Uncle Doc gave me a silver dollar to spend in California."

"Bless his heart," Mother said.

"You can't beat Uncle Doc and Aunt Loula," my father said. "She raised me, you know."

"I thought your grandparents did."

"After they died, I went to live with Aunt Loula and Uncle Doc," he said. "She was like a mother to me."

"I think you love her more than your own mother," I said.

"Maybe I do," he said. "Maybe I do."

There was a pause and we listened to the music coming from the flats.

"Have my brothers gone to bed?"

"Yes. They said to tell you good night. They'll tell you good-bye in the morning," my mother answered.

I was up by seven the next morning with a feeling one moment of exhilaration and the next of sadness. I had breakfast with my brothers and my father, and then he said he had to go to work and my brothers had to go to school. He kissed me good-bye, and I hugged my brothers. I went to the front door and watched them leave the yard and walk in opposite directions, my brothers to their school and my father to his store. I watched until they were out of sight and then I went into my bedroom. My suitcase, packed and ready to go, was on my bed. Tom Brooks had already brought some of his things into the room. I thought, he'll be sleeping in here tonight.

"Where will I sleep when I come home?" I called out to my mother. She didn't answer.

"Mother, where will I sleep when I come home this summer?"

"You'll sleep in your room."

"Where will Tom Brooks sleep?"

"He'll go back again with Johnny."

I went through the bathroom to her room. She was in front of the mirror, combing her hair. She began to cry when she saw me.

"Mama, don't, please."

"I'm sorry. It's just that we'll miss you."

"I'll miss you too."

"And California seems so far away."

"I'll be back for the summer."

"I know. I wish we could bring you home for Christmas, but we can't afford it."

"I know."

"Aunt Mag says she'll have you for Thanksgiving and Mama says she may go to California for Christmas to visit Aunt Bo, and you'll spend Christmas with them."

"Where," I asked, "in Calexico?"

"No, La Jolla. Aunt Bo spends Christmas there. You'll have a good time with her."

"I'm sure."

"You'll like Aunt Bo. She's very beautiful and a lot of fun."

"Do you really think Baboo will come to California for Christmas?"

"I think so. She wants to get away from the boys for a while."

"Where will they go?"

"The boys?"

"Yes."

"They'll be here with us, I guess."

"Mama, what's going to happen to them?"

"I don't know, Son. I ask that every day of my life." I gave her a hug then and went to get my suitcase.

"We'd better go," I said.

"I think so."

When we got to my grandmother's, she and Billy were waiting for us by the car. Billy took my suitcase and put it in the backseat and I embraced my grandmother.

"Good-bye, Baboo."

"Good-bye, Son."

Billy and Mother got in the front seat of the car and I got in the back. Billy backed the car out of the yard into the road, and I turned to wave good-bye to my grandmother. She was crying. I turned away, because I couldn't bear seeing her cry.

Billy was singing to himself: "I'll be glad when you're dead you rascal you."

I looked at him and he seemed very sad to me.

"Thank you for driving me to Houston, Billy," I said.

"That's all right. I'm glad to do it."

He went back to his singing.

I turned around and looked out the window to get one last look at my grandmother and her house, but they were already out of sight. We crossed the Santa Fe tracks. I could see the start of the cotton fields up ahead, and the workers who were already in the fields.

"My Lord, how can they stand to pick cotton in this heat?" my mother asked.

"Brother picked cotton one year in Arizona," Billy said. "Speed was dying to go out to Arizona to join him, but when he heard he was picking cotton, he decided to stay home."

"I remember," Mother said.

We passed Mr. Billy Neal's house.

"Is Mr. Billy Neal still alive, Sister?" Billy asked.

"My heavens, isn't it terrible, I don't know," my mother said.

"I used to see him ride by Baboo's house on his horse going to town, when I was a kid," I said. "I always wanted to ask him to give me a ride, but I never had the nerve."

"He would have given it to you. He was always a friendly soul," Mother said.

"Someone told me he slept with his coffin under his bed," I said.

"I heard that too," Mother said.

"Mrs. Willford kept Mr. Willford's ashes on her mantelpiece, I always heard," Billy said. "And when you came to see her she'd point and say, There's Papa up there."

"I heard that too," Mother said. "We've had a lot of characters in this town."

"Mrs. Willford got kind of peculiar towards the end, you know," I said. "She said it was her duty before she died to teach the men in Wharton to act like gentlemen, and so whenever she met a man uptown who didn't tip his hat and say, how are you today, Mrs. Willford, I hope well, she would take her walking stick and hit him."

I began to laugh thinking of it.

"Daddy was scared of her, you know. If he was standing in front of the store and saw her coming down the sidewalk, he'd go back in the back and tell me to call him after she passed by."

We were passing Peach Creek now, hardly a trickle this time of year. There were pecan trees on its banks, and ropelike grapevines hanging from their branches.

"That's where I broke my arm during the Methodist picnic," Billy said.

"How did you do that?" I asked.

"Don't you remember it?"

"No," I said.

"I climbed a pecan tree and got hold of one of the grapevines and began swinging out from the tree, and the vine broke and I fell to the ground and broke my arm. Remember, Sister?"

"Yes, I do."

"Were you there, Mother?" I asked.

"Yes," she said.

"Was I there?"

"Yes, you were."

"How old was I?"

"Let's see." A pause as she thought it over. "Papa was alive. I guess you were three or four."

"I was nine when he died."

"I was thinking last night," Billy said, "Papa's been dead seven years. I was in school when I got the news he was dead."

"Who told you?" I asked.

"Mr. Autrey. Do you remember him?"

"Yes," I said. "I had him in civics class. And he said one day in civics class when Al Smith was running for president, he didn't know whether to vote for him or Herbert Hoover, and then he thought, what would Papa do if he were alive, and he thought, why, he would vote for Al Smith, Catholic or not, and that's what he did. I wonder why Al Smith opposed Roosevelt so bitterly. Roosevelt supported him when he ran. Why do you think, Mother?"

"Oh, I don't know, Son. I know it made your daddy sick when he heard what he was going to do," she said.

"They called Al Smith the Happy Warrior, didn't they?"

"Do you remember Papa?" Billy asked me.

"Sure, I remember Papa," I said. "Why didn't you let me go to the funeral, Mother?" I asked.

"We thought you were too young," she said.

We rode on in silence. I tried to recall what Papa looked like and what he sounded like. I kept seeing the picture of him Mother had on her dresser. I heard my great-aunt Loula say once she didn't think it was a very good likeness, but everyone else did. Everyone always spoke of his jolly laugh. I couldn't remember how his laugh sounded, or how he sounded when he talked. I remembered that he always had a red bandanna handkerchief and that he blew his nose a lot with great vigor.

"Mama doesn't go to the graveyard like she used to," Billy said.

"Seven years," Mother said. "Is it possible?"

There was silence again then and I looked around at the fields.

"Did we pass Kendleton?" I asked.

"Back a ways," Mother said.

Only blacks lived in Kendleton, and it had only one store.

"How large is Kendleton?" I asked.

"I have no idea, Son. Do you know, Billy?"

"No," Billy said.

"Take a guess," I said.

"Maybe a hundred people, wouldn't you say, Sister?"

"Maybe so. I really wouldn't know."

"Have you ever been to Kendleton?" I asked.

"No," my mother said. "Just to pass through like we did today."

"Have you, Billy?" I asked.

"No. There's a white family that lives there now. They own the general store."

"Was that the store Oliver Ray's grandfather had when the colored man shot and killed him?"

"No, I don't think so," Mother said. "I think that happened in Peach Creek."

Again Billy began to sing to himself: "I'll be glad when you're dead you rascal you."

"They play that recording by Louis Armstrong all the time in the barbecue joints in the flats," I said. "Do you like Louie Armstrong, Billy?"

"I do," he said.

"That time you played the saxophone and sang at the Methodist tea, Rita Doris told me she thought you sang better than Rudy Vallee."

"Yeah," Billy said. "Maybe I'll be a singer."

He took a pack of cigarettes out of his pocket and offered the pack to me.

"Want a cigarette?"

"Thank you," I said, taking one. I reached in my pocket for a match to light my cigarette as Billy lit his.

"Remember that time, Sister, when Tom Brooks went away with the Boy Scouts on the coast and a hurricane was reported on its way and Lloyd Rust and Big Horton went to get Tom Brooks and Lloyd's boy, what's his name?" Billy asked.

"Lloyd, Jr.," Mother said.

"Sure, that's right," Billy said. "And coming back there were heavy rains and strong winds and Big Horton was in front with Lloyd and Lloyd wanted to light a cigarette and he asked Big Horton to hold the wheel while he lit a cigarette and Big Horton had never done that before and he was nervous and drove the car into a ditch."

Billy is laughing now and Mother is laughing too. I was trying to visualize what it was like in the rain and the wind, when my father drove the car into the ditch.

"Lloyd never let him forget it, you know," Mother said. "He still teases him about it."

"Why hasn't he ever had a car, Sister?"

"Because we can't afford it."

"He could afford it," Billy said.

"He doesn't think so," Mother said.

"Mama wanted to give you-all a car, she told me, but Big Horton wouldn't let her."

"I know."

"Would you like a car, Mother?" I asked.

"Maybe one day," she said.

Billy began singing to himself again, this time "Stardust," when he suddenly stopped.

"Sister."

"Yes, Billy."

"You're disappointed in me, aren't you?"

"You are a very smart man, Billy. I just wish you'd realize that."

Again there was silence. Billy threw his cigarette out the window and I rolled my window down and threw my cigarette out too.

"I never wanted to be a lawyer," he said. "It was Papa that was always talking about it, and always going on what a brilliant lawyer Uncle Billy was and I would have to work hard to ever be as good as he was."

My mother said nothing and there was silence again. It made

me uncomfortable and I tried to think of something to talk about.

"Are we in Fort Bend County now?" I asked.

"Been in Fort Bend for a while. That's Rosenberg coming up."

"Then Richmond," I said.

"Yes," Billy said, and continued. "At Richmond there's a drive-in before you cross the bridge. I want to stop for a Coke."

I looked at my mother. She was looking out the window. Again I tried to think of something to talk about.

"Aunt Lida's friend Miss Inez Darst lives in Richmond," I said.

"Yes," Mother said.

"She is Aunt Lida's closest friend, Aunt Lida told me."

"Yes," Mother said. "I expect so."

"Aunt Lida says they have lost all their money and she has to bake cakes to make ends meet."

"I know," Mother said.

"Was Miss Inez very rich?" I asked.

"I guess so. That's what everybody says, but I really wouldn't know," Mother said. "There are some very rich people in Richmond. I know that. The old families, you know."

"Richer than people in Wharton?" I asked.

"I don't know if they're richer, but they spend money in ways Wharton people don't."

"Wharton people are a bunch of mossbacks," Billy said.

"I don't know about that, Billy," Mother said. "They just don't believe in throwing their money away on frivolous things."

When we got to the Richmond River Bridge, Billy pulled up to the drive-in and parked.

"Do you want a Coke, Sister?" he asked.

"Yes," she said, "and I want to treat."

A waitress came up to the car.

"What will it be?" she asked.

"Three Cokes," Billy said. "A lot of ice in mine."

"Yessir," the girl said, and went for the Cokes.

"Well, there's no turning back now," I said.

"What do you mean by that, Son?" Mother asked.

"I mean I couldn't go back now even if I wanted to. People in Wharton would never let me forget it."

"Do you not want to, Son?"

"Do I not want to what?"

"Go to California, Son."

"No. I want to go. But even if I didn't I'd make myself since Daddy has paid the money."

The waitress came back with the Cokes on a tray. She put the tray on the car window, and Billy handed Cokes to Mother and to me.

"Anything else?" the waitress asked.

"No, thank you," Mother said.

"How much?" Billy asked.

"Fifteen cents," the waitress said.

Mother opened her purse and took out fifteen cents and handed it to the waitress.

"Thank you, ma'm," the waitress said, and went back to the drive-in.

"She's pretty," Billy said.

"In New York Virginia Neff told me that you tip waitresses," I said.

"Even carhops?" Billy asked.

"Everybody," I said.

We finished our Cokes and Billy honked the horn and the waitress came out for the tray.

"You're pretty, miss. Did anybody ever tell you that?"

"No, sir," the waitress said, blushing.

"Well, you are," Billy said.

"Thank you, sir," she said, and took the tray back into the drive-in. Billy offered me another cigarette, which I took. He lit one for himself and then held the match for me to light mine.

"Thanks, Billy," I said.

Mother looked at her watch.

"We'd better be on our way, Billy."

"OK, Sister," he said.

He started the car and headed again for the highway.

"Thanks for the Coke," he said.

"Yeah, thanks, Mom," I said.

"You have your bus ticket, honey?" she asked.

"Yes, ma'm."

"And your wallet?"

"Yes, ma'm."

Up ahead were the cotton fields of the state prison farm. Convicts could be seen working in the fields, two guards on horseback watching over them.

"Poor devils," Mother said as we passed.

"Do you remember when the Pierce estate worked convicts?" I asked.

"I do," Billy said. "We called it the prison farm then. Instead of the Pierce estate paying the convicts it paid the state."

"Did the state pay the convicts?" I wanted to know.

"I doubt it. Not much anyway," Billy said.

Up ahead was the town of Sugar Land with its sugar refinery. At one time this part of the state had acres and acres in sugarcane.

"Daddy says in another five or ten years there won't be any sugarcane growing in Wharton County or Fort Bend County. He says we can't compete with the cheap Louisiana and Cuban labor," I said.

I looked up at Mother and Billy for a response. They both seemed very preoccupied and I don't think they had even heard me.

We got to the Houston bus station a half hour before my bus was to leave. Big Mama and Aunt Lily were waiting for us in the station, and I saw Mother stiffen when she saw Aunt Lily. She never discussed her with me, but I knew she didn't like her. As a matter of fact, I think Lily was the only person in this world that she didn't like. She liked Big Mama even though she knew my daddy in his heart (as she told me once) had never forgiven her for abandoning him as a child. I knew my aunt Lily didn't like my mother either for she told me once that it was a great sorrow to her that she couldn't get close to my mother, as she had never had a sister, and she had so hoped when her brother married he would marry someone she could feel close to, someone who could be a sister to her.

I looked at my mother and I looked at Aunt Lily. My mother had just turned thirty-nine and her hair was turning gray. I thought of the day she bobbed her hair. Bobbed hair was just coming in fashion when she decided to try it. My father was all for it, but she was afraid Papa wouldn't approve. I remembered when she came home after she'd had it done and how different she looked. It was late afternoon and she took me by the hand

and we started for my grandparents' house, when Papa appeared in the yard, and when he saw her he stopped and said, "My God, Hallie, what in the world have you done to yourself?"

"Do you like it, Papa?" she said.

"You want the truth?"

"Yessir."

"Well, I don't like it very much, but I suppose I'll get used to it. There a lot of things I don't like that I finally get used to."

My mother had put on her best dress for the trip to Houston, and I could see Aunt Lily looking at the dress. I remembered that Big Mama (who had made her living as a seamstress when she first came to Houston) had made it for her. Several times a year she made dresses for Mother, always cautioning her not to tell Aunt Lily, as Aunt Lily was jealous of anything she did for Mother. For me, too, apparently, because once when I was visiting her in Houston and she bought me a pair of tennis shoes she asked me not to tell Aunt Lily she had given them to me.

Aunt Lily was a year older than Mother and her hair was dyed and she had a permanent.

"Hallie," she said. "You're getting gray."

"Yes, I am."

"It runs in her family," my grandmother said. "Daisy was gray by the time she was forty. We'd be gray, too, honey, if we didn't dye our hair."

"Not me, Mama, I'm a natural blonde. Blondes don't gray. Is Brother getting gray, Hallie?"

"No," my mother said.

Big Mama, obviously wanting to change the subject, turned the attention to me.

"Come give your Big Mama a hug and a kiss, Sonny."

She held out her arms and I went over and she hugged and kissed me.

"Now, hold out your hand," she said.

I did so and she put a five-dollar bill in my hand.

"Oh, thank you," I said, and kissed her again.

"Put it in your wallet, darling," Mother said.

I took out my wallet and put the five dollars in it and put the wallet back in my pocket.

"How are you, Billy?" Aunt Lily asked.

"Pretty fair, thank you, Lily."

"Guess what's happened to me?" Aunt Lily said. "The Houston Woman's Club has invited me to come and play my compositions for them. I was so thrilled when they called to tell me. And I was so inspired by their interest in my work that I sat down last Thursday and composed two more pieces. I called the president of the club, a lovely lady, and I said I have a surprise for you. What is it? she said. I have written two pieces especially for the event. Oh, Mrs. Coffee, you are just unbelievable," she said.

"Well," my mother said.

"What are the names of your pieces?" Billy asked.

"One is called 'Stillness,' and the other's called 'Heartbroken,' " she said.

"And beautiful they are too," Big Mama said. "They are songs, you know."

"The first songs I've written in a long, long time," Aunt Lily said. "The soloist at our church has agreed to sing them at the recital. She says she finds them very impressive."

Billy looked at his watch.

"We'd better get you to the bus, Little Horton."

"They'll call out when the bus is ready," Aunt Lily said.

Just then the bus to Dallas was announced. Billy picked up my suitcase.

"I can carry it, Billy," I said.

"No, I'll carry it."

I started for the bus, my mother, Aunt Lily, my grandmother and Billy following.

"Got your ticket, Son?" Mother asked.

"Yes, ma'm."

"Better get it out."

"Yes, ma'm."

I took my ticket out of my inside coat pocket, and I heard someone crying behind me. I looked around and it was Big Mama.

"Now, Mama," Aunt Lily said, "you promised me you wouldn't give way to your feelings."

"I know," she said. "But he's going so far away."

"I'll be back this summer, Big Mama."

I went over to her and tried to comfort her. The bus driver called: "All aboard."

"Well, this it," I said.

I began to choke up and knew I had better get on the bus before I started crying, so I quickly kissed my aunt Lily, shook Billy's hand, kissed my grandmother Cleveland and then my mother and headed for the bus. The bus was crowded, but I was able to get a seat by a window that enabled me to see them. Mother was crying now, too, and Billy was comforting her and Aunt Lily was comforting Big Mama.

The bus driver got in his seat, closed the door, started the engine and I began to wave good-bye. Mother was somewhat composed by now, but Big Mama was crying uncontrollably.

The bus started pulling out of the station. I waved to them again and they waved back, and we were soon in the street and I kept looking back, until I couldn't see them anymore.

My aunt Laura met me in Dallas and we drove right away to her house. She began asking me a million questions about our family in Wharton. She had just gotten a letter from my grandmother about Billy walking away from practicing law, and she was upset, of course. She asked about Speed and Brother, and I told her what I knew, which really wasn't very much. But she kept talking about them, going over the past and all their misdeeds, every once in a while saying what in the name of heavens is going to become of them. Finally she turned to me as if I knew the answer and said, "Where will it all end? Little Horton, where will it all end?"

The next morning she took me to the Dallas bus station and she insisted on going inside the station with me. I hoped she wouldn't cry as I was leaving, and she didn't. She stood waving to me as the bus pulled away.

I was seated next to a plain girl, shabbily dressed, who kept opening and closing her purse. She seemed very nervous. I hoped if she, too, was going all the way to California, she wouldn't continue opening and closing her purse. By the time we had left Dallas and were out in the country, she had stopped. She turned to me and smiled.

"Are you going to California?" she asked.

"Yes, I am."

"Did you ever hear of James Hall?"

"James Hall?"

"He's a movie star."

"Sure, I know that."

"Have you ever seen any of his pictures?"

"Yes. And I have a cousin that collects movie star pictures, and she has one of his."

"Is it autographed?"

"I think so."

"What pictures of his have you seen?" she asked.

I couldn't remember exactly, but before I said that she continued talking.

"He's my brother."

"Oh, is he? Well . . ."

"I'm going out to visit him."

"Oh, you are?"

"Yes, and I may stay on. I'll see how I like it when I get there. Are you going on a visit?"

"No, I'm going to school."

"What kind of school?"

"Acting school in Pasadena."

"Oh."

There was a pause then, and she looked out the window and then back at me.

"My brother doesn't believe in acting schools. He doesn't think acting can be taught."

"Oh?"

"Yes, that's what he told me. He never went to acting school." A pause, then, "You want to get into the movies?"

"No, I want to be a stage actor."

"Oh. If you wanted to get into the movies, I would introduce you to my brother."

We stopped at another bus stop to pick up more passengers.

She was looking out the window again, so I could get a look at her without her noticing. She didn't look like James Hall, I thought, and why would James Hall's sister be riding a bus to California instead of a train and why would she be dressed the way she was? The bus started on its way again and she began talking about Hollywood, and the friends of her brother, and how Buddy Rogers was her favorite actor and her brother was going to see to it she met him.

I hadn't slept well the night before from all the excitement over leaving and so I fell to sleep while she was talking. When I woke up it was night, and she was asleep. I looked out the window and I had no idea where we were. I wondered if we were still in Texas. Wherever it was, I could tell we were in the country, and it was pitch black outside and not even any stars. I checked my wallet in case a pickpocket had taken it while I was asleep, but it was still there.

I looked at my wristwatch and it was ten-thirty. I thought of my family, my mother and father sitting on the front porch probably talking about me and wondering where I was now. I thought of my brothers and I imagined that Tom Brooks was in my room asleep. I thought of the drugstores in Wharton about to close for the night. I thought of saying good-bye to my mother, Aunt Lily, my grandmother and Billy in the bus station.

James Hall's sister began to snore. I heard other people snoring in the bus. I looked out the window again. There were a few stars now. I closed my eyes, and the doubts began again. What if you have no talent, what if you finish acting school and you can't find a job acting and you have to go back home and work at your father's store the rest of your life? What if . . . Hush up, I said to myself, just hush up. There is no going back now. I closed my eyes then, and I thought of Billy singing, "I'll be glad when you're dead you rascal you," and I wondered for the millionth time what would become of Billy and Speed and Brother. The tune of "I'll be glad when you're dead you rascal you" came into my head then and I was listening to it as I went back to sleep.